Fundamentals of
Patents and Patenting

Covers PCI M. Pharma Syllabii
Law Syllabii on IPR & Patents Law
and Patent Agent Exams

Fundamentals of
Patents and Patenting

Covers PCI M. Pharma Syllabii
Law Syllabii on IPR & Patents Law
and Patent Agent Exams

Dr. Vivekananda Mandal

[Former WERC Researcher, Govt. of Japan]
Assistant Professor
Division of Pharmacognosy
Department of Pharmacy
Guru Ghasidas Vishwavidyalaya
(A Central University)
Bilaspur (CG) 495009
India

Mr. Kavi Bhushan Singh Chouhan

Senior Research Fellow
Division of Pharmacognosy
Department of Pharmacy
Guru Ghasidas Vishwavidyalaya
(A Central University)
Bilaspur (CG) 495009
India

BSP BS Publications
A unit of **BSP Books Pvt., Ltd.**
4-4-309/316, Giriraj Lane,
Sultan Bazar, Hyderabad - 500 095

Fundamentals of Patents and Patenting
by Vivekananda Mandal and Kavi Bhushan Singh Chouhan

Published by:

BSP **BS Publications**
A unit of **BSP Books Pvt. Ltd.**

4-4-309/316, Giriraj Lane, Sultan Bazar,
Hyderabad - 500 095
Phone: 040 - 23445688
e-mail : info@bspbooks.net
www.bspbooks.net

ISBN: 978-93-91910-17-4

Dedicated to

Frontline corona warriors and to those Innovators who made our life easy during COVID-19 pandemic

Preface

In the current era, technology and digitization is seen as a new dimension which has become an integral part of our life. Having said this, intellectual property (IP) which is the root cause of the current outburst in technological advancement becomes the most wanted tool for societal and economic development of a country. Arms and ammunition are no more considered as power exhibitors of a country, rather it is the IP asset of a country which makes it a super power. Having realized the enormous potential of IP assets, several countries have started building up their ecosystem which can breed innovations in a sustainable way and then creating favourable legislations in compliance with various international treaties so that such innovations can be made full use of for strengthening the economy of the country.

India too is a global breeding ground for innovation. The national IPR policy have rightly addressed all those needs which are required to make India one of the global leaders in innovation. Creating an innovation doesn't end the journey but rather it is the beginning as the innovator should be competent enough in seeking protection of his innovation, protect the innovation from infringements by enforcing his IP rights and also should be able to commercialize his innovation. Resonating with the National IPR policy, the authors have strategically presented a simplified version of patents and patenting in India. The book is expected to serve as a capacity building tool for young innovators, particularly lesser visible innovators in developing a simplified deeper understanding in protecting their innovations. The book is a dedicated source of knowledge regarding patents and patenting in India and shall cover everything from cradle to grave regarding all aspects of patenting in India. The book shall serve as a one stop destination for University students, research scholars and law students in understanding patents and fundamentals of patenting which the authors believe shall satisfy their curriculum needs as well. Moreover, research scholars are often ignorant about their innovations and seems to be more inclined towards obtaining publications which obviously kills further patenting scope. This book shall be an eye opener as it is committed towards elimination of patent ignorance. The book shall also be useful to aspirants who are preparing for patent agent examination, industry personnel's and educators in the field of IPR. The book has been organized into 20 chapters highlighting every aspect of patents and patenting in India with special address to PCT filing and international treaties. The wisely framed FAQ's answers most of the doubts arising in the mind of young innovators particularly University students and researchers.

The foundation of the book was laid amid the COVID-19 lockdown period. The authors have used the lockdown period in channelizing their positive energy for the betterment of the society by disseminating their knowledge in the form of this book. The authors wish to thank their family members for their support during the hardships faced in the lockdown period. Staying united for a cause was the 'mantra' behind surviving as a unit in the lockdown crisis. The authors also wish to thank the frontline corona warriors whose tiresome efforts kept us safe and healthy. The authors finally wish everybody a healthy and happy learning experience with this book.

- *Authors*

Contents

CHAPTER 1

Overview of Indian Patent System

1.1 Pre-Independence Scenario

The history of patent legislation in India has a huge British influence because making of the legislation started during the British rule. The first evidence of such legislation in India can be found in 1856 as the 'Act of VI', adopted from the British law of 1852 with minor modifications. This particular legislation was based on encouraging new and useful innovations and also to motivate inventors to disclose such innovations for the benefit of the society. Since competent approval of the British Crown was not obtained for the enactment of this law in India, hence it was deemed to be revoked and was then replaced by the 'Act IX' of 1857. Then came the 'Act XV' of 1859 which was much appreciated for the inclusion of 'exclusive privilege' rights, which allowed selling and using the invention in India by the inventor himself or by any authorized persons for a term of 14 years. This act was seen as a drastic improvement in protecting the rights of the inventor as it increased the radius of 'exclusive privilege' from useful inventions to all types of inventions and extension of priority period from 6 months to 12 months. Novelty of invention and prior public use of the said invention in India or United Kingdom was considered before granting of such privileges. The act of 1859 was re-thought in 1872 and its inclusiveness was increased by integrating protection of designs and thus was renamed accordingly as 'The Patterns and Designs Protection Act' under 'Act XIII' of 1872. More amendments were made in 1883 which was known as 'Act XVI' of 1883. Such amendments were made in light of the fact that those inventions which were exhibited at the Calcutta International Exhibition World's fair, before filing of application seeking patent protection, shall not loose novelty if filed for protection within 6 months from the opening date of such exhibitions. This rule formed the basis of modern Indian patents act clause 'Not Anticipations' mentioned under Section 29-34. In order to be in tandem with the British law prevailing in United Kingdom, some changes were incorporated in the Indian law in light of the changes made in Britain in the year 1883. Such changes were officially inducted into the Indian law in 1888. Some noticeable changes that were inducted to be in resonance with the changes made in Britain were,

- Extensions of jurisdiction
- Fee reduction
- Extension of exclusive privileges
- To call for a model of the invention for the purpose of examination
- Appointment of agents to facilitate filing process for seeking patent protection
- Grant of compulsory license

Finally, the Indian Patents and Designs Act came to existence in 1911 which was the most comprehensive act on patents and designs to have existed before independence. With the enforcement of this act all other previous acts ceased to exist. Many of the provisions regarding patent administration and patent processing that are currently mentioned in the existing act of 1970 owes its existence from the 1911 act. Subsequent amendments made in 1920, 1930 and 1945 lead to the incorporation of several currently existing provisions such as establishment of Controller of Patents for administering the patents act, patent of addition, government powers to take control of certain inventions, concept of provisional specification etc.

1.2 Post-Independence Scenario

The Indian Patents Act, 1970 was metamorphosed to its current stage through the extensive reviews and recommendations given by two expert committees namely,

(a) Justice (Dr.) Bakshi Tek Chand Committee

(b) Justice N. Rajagopala Ayyangar Committee

Justice (Dr.) Bakshi Tek Chand Committee: Due to the dynamic nature of our society and rapidly changing configuration of the economic & political environment of our country, an urgent need was felt to hyphenate the existing patent system to such changing environment. In order to achieve this task, Government constituted the Justice (Dr.) Bakshi Tek Chand Committee in 1949.The said committee was expected to review the then existing patent legislation and provide deeper inside into various aspects like prevention of abuse of patent rights, implementation of special provisions to govern patents on food/medicine, provision to regulate patent agents, provisions on best practices of patent office and services rendered by them etc. The recommendations by the committee were submitted on 04.08.1949. The committee suggested certain amendments in some sections of the then existing act to prevent abuse of patent rights, through grant of compulsory license, revocation of patent and setting up an ad-hoc special tribunal with judiciary powers to provide relief against abuse of patent rights. The committee also emphasized the need of making inventions related to food, medicine, surgical devices available to the public at an affordable price with suitable compensation to the patentee as well. Some of the recommendations of the committee was incorporated in the patent act in 1950, particularly those related to compulsory license and revocation as it was very necessary to prevent abuse of patent rights at the earliest. However, when the bill was introduced in the Parliament in 1953 (the first Lok Sabha after independence), it lapsed as the government did not press hard enough to get it passed by the parliament.

Justice N. Rajagopala Ayyangar Committee: After the independence, the primary objective of the government was to make the country self-sustainable on social, economic and technological grounds. Henceforth, to achieve this task it was clear that the country's economy needs a continuous infusion of inventions which shall indirectly benefit the society as well. On the other hand, abuses related to patent rights also needs to be curbed which otherwise could be a discouraging factor for the society. In light of the above facts, it was very necessary to bring a huge reform in the then existing Patents and Design Act, 1950 and hence the Justice N. Rajagopala Ayyangar Committee was constituted in 1957 to examine the question of revision of the patent law and suggest the government accordingly. The committee extensively studied the Swan committee report of the UK and also went through the recommendations of various other committees constituted by different countries for bringing reforms in their patent act. The said Ayyangar committee understood the evils of monopoly which a patent provides but also realized the goodness of technological and innovation stimulation that the patent system provides to the society. Thus, the patent system was not only to provide monopoly advantage to the patentee but also to bring technological advancement by providing inventors a conducive environment for inventions which shall largely play a critical role in the economic development of the country. Ayyangar committee's major role was to get this balance of patent monopoly and technological advancement right for a sustainable economic and social development of the country. Ayyangar committee took a note of the fact that an Indian patentee should take all efforts to commercialize the invention in India, the committee also noted that conclusive evidence is available to prove the fact that countries who have adopted patent system have witnessed significant technological advancement. Henceforth, the committee recommended retention of the patent system in India along with some major changes in the patent act. This is was when the existing Patent Act, 1970 was taking its final shape. The currently prevailing patent legislation in the form of Indian Patents Act, 1970 came into existence when the bill was passed through a Joint Parliamentary Committee. The said act replaced all other previously prevailing legislation. The provisions of the act mostly came into force on 20th April, 1972 along with patent Rules, 1972. Some of the then salient features of the act were,

- Classifying certain inventions as non-patentable
- Foreign filing rules for Indian resident
- Provisions for imposing secrecy directions for inventions related to defence purposes of the country
- Expansion of scope of patent revocation
- Provision of further appeal to High Court against specific decisions of the Controller
- Expansion of Indian patent office
- Strengthening of compulsory licensing

An illustrative representation depicting the various events associated with the birth of Indian Patents Act, 1970 along with time line is given below for easy understanding of the proceedings.

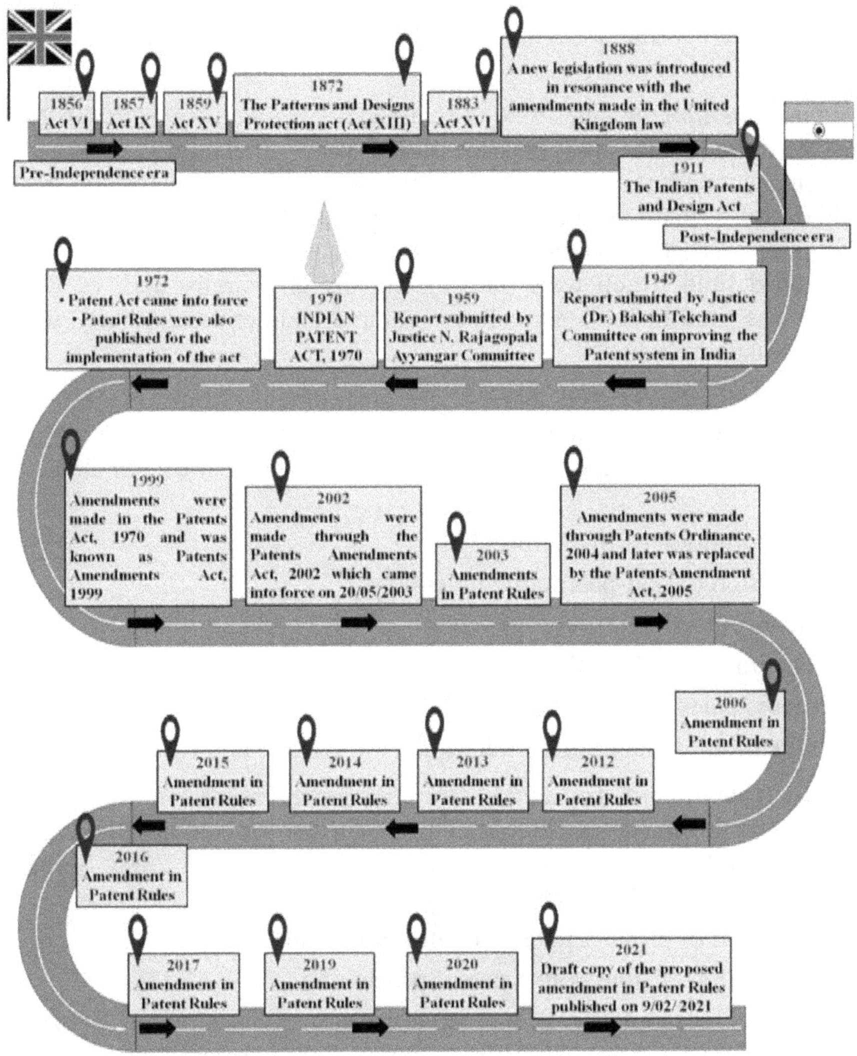

FIGURE 1.1 History of Indian patent system along with time line.

Patent Amendments

Three major amendments were made to the Patents Act, 1970. The first amendment is known as the Patents Amendment Act, 1999, the second is known as the Patents Amendment Act, 2002 and the third is known as Patents Amendment Act, 2005. For the implementation of the patents act, patent rules were published in 1972 which also underwent a series of amendments which shall be described separately in the next section. All these amendments were made to comply with the minimum protection and patent administration standards laid down by TRIPS agreement to which India became a signatory in 1995. The amendments made are briefly described below,

***Patents Amendment Act, 1999*:** The amendments were approved in 1999 and was made effective retrospectively from 1st January 1995. This particular amendment made way for the filing of product patents in the field of drugs, pharmaceuticals and agricultural chemicals. It also allowed Exclusive marketing Rights (EMR) for articles belonging to the above-mentioned field which were patented in foreign country and for which patent was filed in India as well, for commercial activities related to the said products in India

Patents Amendment Act, 2002: these amendments came into force on 20.05.2003 along with the introduction of the new Patent Rules, 2003. Some of the most important amendments that were made in 2002 act were,

- New definition of Invention
- Expansion of non-patentable inventions
- Patent protection term of 20 years
- Constitution of Appellate Board
- Process patent for microorganisms
- Prevention of patenting of traditional knowledge and biodiversity

***Patents Amendment Act, 2005*:** The third amendments were brought in the form of ordinance in 2004 which was further replaced by the Patents Amendment Act, 2005 which came into force from 01.01.2005. Some of the important amendments made were,

- Expansion of product patents to all fields of invention
- Introduction of time bound patent processing
- Grant of compulsory license to export medicines to such foreign countries who have no infrastructure for such production during public health crisis
- Introduction of pre-grant and post-grant opposition

***Patent Rules*:** in order to implement the Patents Act, 1970, government constituted the Patent Rules, 1972 to facilitate implementation and administering the Patent act, 1970. A new set of patent rules were framed in 2003 which replaced the earlier existing rules of 1972. Further amendments to these rules were made in 2005, 2006, 2012, 2013, 2014, 2015, 2016, 2017, 2019, 2020 and 2021. The most important amendments that were made in 2019 were,

- Mandatory for patent agent to operate only through electronic submission of documents

- No transmittal fee for PCT applications filed electronically
- Widening the scope of rule 7 to encourage startups by considering them as small entities

Patent Amendment Rules, 2020 came into force from 19.10.2020, which further streamlined and created ease of operation regarding requirements related to filing Form-27 and submission of verified English translation of priority documents. On February 9th, 2021 Government of India through DPIIT published the draft copy of the proposed patent amendment rules 2021. The proposed rule intends to benefit eligible educational institutions (Indian and Foreign) in terms of filing fee and expediting examination process.

CHAPTER 2

Understanding IPR

Intellectual Property Rights (IPR)

The property or output produced from human creativity using human intellect power, creative ideas, critical thinking and mind power is known as intellectual property. Such output could take the shape of invention which could be patented, designs, symbols used as trademarks, literary works, artistic works, music/dance composition etc. Mankind has always valued tangible movable and immovable properties as symbol of being wealth and financially secured. Such properties are either gained through inheritance or earned in one's lifetime. But with time the world has changed and a new intangible property which can be created through human intellect is now ruling the world. Countries which hold maximum such intellectual property rights is now considered to be stronger and wealthier. When some intellectual property in the form of an invention, design, symbol, artistic work etc. have been created, it is very important for the creator to take ownership of such creations, so that the creator can enjoy complete monopoly of such creations and use it for earning revenue as well. The wide array of legal options which are available for taking ownership of such creations are known collectively as Intellectual Property Rights. Each type of creation can be protected by a specific intellectual property right or in other words one single right is not applicable to all type of creations. For example, in-order to take ownership of an invention, the legal right that is available is 'patent'. For taking ownership of literary works, artistic works the legal option that can be exercised is 'copyright'. Similarly, for every such creation, a specific right can be claimed. Such rights provide exclusive ownership to the creator or any person assigned by the creator for a specific time period. In the said time period of protection, no other person without the consent of the person holding such intellectual property right, cannot use such creations. Unauthorized use of such creations which are protected under a specific intellectual property right can attract legal proceedings. The person holding such right can do whatever normally he could have done if in possession with any tangible movable or immovable property (like land, house or car). This means he can sell, rent or license out the intellectual property to any third party. Such property can also be inherited. Some rights do continue lifelong provided extension has been applied by the person holding the right, while few rights might be restricted to certain time period only. However, after the lapse of such time period, the intellectual property is made open to public and anybody can use the same without the consent of the person who held the right. This chapter shall discuss the various types of intellectual property rights available to the creator of an intellectual property through which one can claim ownership of such creations.

1. ***Patents***: Patent is an exclusive statutory right granted by the Government to the applicant for inventions which could be either a product or process. Such right in the form of patent is granted in lieu of complete disclosure of the invention to the government. The concerned patent office of the country evaluates the disclosure to understand the novelty, inventive step and industrial applicability of the invention. Patent is granted for a fixed time period which is 20 years. Patent is governed through The Patents Act, 1970

2. ***Industrial Designs***: It indicates only feature, shape, configuration, pattern, colour applicable to any article either in two dimensional or three dimensional or both in-order to improve the appearance of the finished product which can be judged only through naked eye. Industrial designs have nothing to do with the quality of the product or content of the packaging but rather indicates the overall look or feel of the product to attract customers and get an extra edge over the competitor's products. Such designs can improve market opportunities of the product by increasing the sale of the product due to the comfort that it provides to the customers owing to its attractive external configuration. Such designs can be registered provided it is not against public order or morality. Any obscene symbol or anything which hurts religious sentiments cannot be used. Governed through The Designs Act, 2000. The total term of protection for a registered design is 15 years, which is granted initially for first 10 years, extendable by another 5 years after the expiry of the initial term of 10 years.

   Example: design of a bottle, design of a LED bulb, design of an container which will provide ease of usage to the user.

3. ***Trademarks***: It is a visual symbol in the form of name, logo and text applied to an article of commerce to indicate either the manufacturer or service provider. Trademark indirectly is an identity of an article and influence the customers purchase decision. Customer sees a mark of respect and reputation for the manufacturer or service provided in the trademark. The manufacturer earns this respect

through the quality of its products over the years and successfully establishes a feeling of trust in the customer's mind. By seeing the trademark, the customer easily recognizes the product from others and based on the reputation and trust on the manufacturer, the customer immediately makes his purchasing decision. Trademarks should be easy to spell and remember and may or may not have a logical relationship with the actual product.

Example: logo of 'Apple' has no resemblance with the actual product and is a well-respected trademark in the field of computers and smart phones. Similarly, logo of manufacturers of shoes, garments, electronic appliances, furniture's, ready to eat food etc. all play an important role in the purchasing decision of the customer. Governed through Trade Marks Act, 1999. Government symbols like Emblem of India, any other obscene or religious symbols (likely to hurt religious sentiments) cannot be used as trademarks.

4. ***Geographical Indication (GI)***: It identifies agricultural or manufactured goods originating from a particular geographical region and having a special characteristic property which makes it different from other products. Such characteristics quality for which it has a special identity from the commercial point of view and creates a sense of interest for its purchase in the customers mind, is due to its origin from a particular geographical region. May be the soil characteristics, climatic condition induces such special quality in the product (if grown agriculturally) or may be the raw materials required for manufacturing the product or the art required for producing the product is only available with the local people of that region.

   Example: Nagpur oranges, Darjeeling tea, Mysore sandal wood soap, Mysore silk, Kancheepuram silk, Kolhapur chappals etc. The quality present in Assam Tea or Darjeeling Tea may not be present in tea grown in other places like Ooty or Munnar because the climatic and soil conditions of Assam induce special flavor and taste which is not present in other tea varieties grown in different places.

   Such right is given to a cooperative society or may be to a group of farmers but not given to any individual. Assigning such right promotes commerce and trade associated with such products and prevents unauthorized sale of duplicated products from other regions. Governed by Geographical Indication of Goods Act 1999. The term of a GI shall be for a period of 10 years but may be renewed from time to time for an unlimited period by payment of renewal fees.

5. ***Semiconductor Integrated Circuit Layout Design***: Semiconductor integrated circuits layout design act 2000 provides protection for semiconductor IC layout and designs. Semiconductor IC consists of a certain arrangement of transistors along with other circuitry elements connected with wires in an inseparable manner on a semiconductor material to carry out a specific circuitry function which is visible as an electronic output. The duration of protection under this right is for 10 years after the first commercial exploitation, provided such exploitation takes place within 5 years from the year of its creation, or 15 years from the year of its creation. For registering such IC layout designs, it should be new and not commercially exploited before anywhere in India or in any convention country.
6. ***Plant Variety Protection Act***: Governed by Protection of Plant Variety and Farmers Rights Act, 2001. New variety of plants which are produced through transgenic methods or asexual reproduction can be protected under this act by any breeder or any University. For a new variety there should be one essential characteristic available in the said variety which is clearly distinguishable from other varieties. Such characteristics should be uniformly expressed in such plants and should remain unchanged in all subsequent generations. Registration is not possible for those varieties which are harmful to public, maintained as non-registerable by government and produced by terminator technology (seeds can be grown and cultivated once, seeds obtained after first generation are sterile and cannot be used for further cultivation). Registration is valid for 18 years in case of vine and trees and for 15 years for others.
7. ***Copyright***: It is a type of protection which covers both published and unpublished literary, scientific and artistic work. It also includes dramatic, musical work along with artistic creations like paintings, photographs, cinematographic work, sound recording etc. Such protection comes into existence as soon as the work is created and formal registration is always not required. Formal registration may be required in case there is a legal battle regarding who created the work first. Unauthorized copying of other literary and such works shall amount to infringement which is often known as plagiarism. Thesis submitted at University level for the award of a particular degree is checked for plagiarism before submission to prevent unauthorized copying from external sources. Governed by the India Copyright Act, 1957. As a general rule, for works created after 1st January 1978, copyright protection lasts for the life of the author plus an additional 70 years. The time span is 50 years from the end of the calendar year in which it was created for sound recordings and broadcasts.

CHAPTER 3

Patent Terminologies

3.1 Invention

Patents are granted for an invention. An invention as per Section 2(1) (j) of Indian Patents Act is defined as a new product or process involving an inventive step and capable of industrial application.

3.2 Priority Date

It is the date on which a patent application is filed for the first time in any country. This date is of great legal significance because if anything similar to the invention which has been filed for patenting is found to exist in the public domain before the priority date, it could then destroy the novelty of the invention thus weakening the probability of getting a patent on the said invention. In simpler words, if any patent literature similar to the filed patent application is available before the priority date or any other similar records published and available in public domain before the priority date of a patent application, will be considered as a prior art and may be enough to invalidate the filed patent application (refer figure 3.1 given below for better understanding).

If several researchers or companies are working on a particular problem trying to find out a solution in the form of an invention, then the company which reserves a priority date by filing the patent application first will win the race of getting a patent for that particular invention. Companies filing patent for the similar invention after the priority date will not be eligible for getting a patent. Priority date can be lost and maintained as well. When an invention is not yet completed and conclusive data related to the invention have not yet been generated, in such situation to stay ahead in the race of getting a patent, a provisional application can be filed for reserving a priority date. However, in the said situation the priority date can be maintained by the applicant only when the complete application is filed within 12 months of filing the provisional application, otherwise the priority date advantage is lost. Priority date can also be

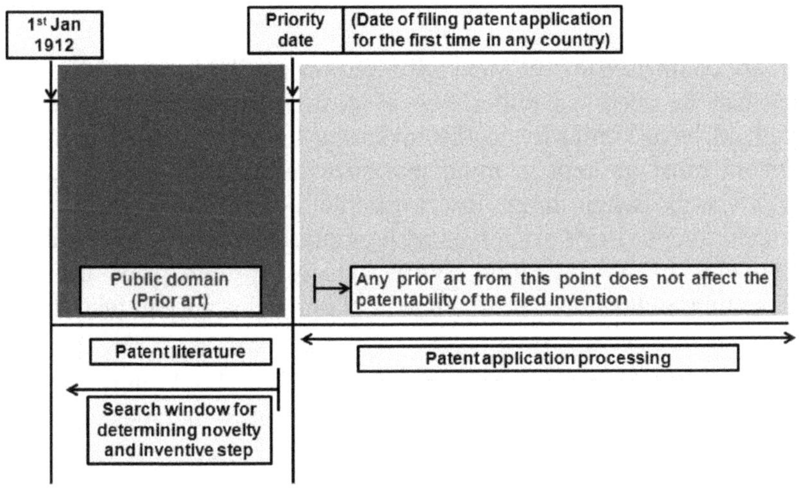

FIGURE 3.1 Illustrative representation of priority date.

maintained if within 12 months from the priority date, patent filing is done (PCT/international filing) in convention countries. For example, if priority date for an application filed in India is 1st January 2020, then the applicant(s) will get this same priority date for all international filings (in countries which are members of Paris Convention only) and PCT filings if the filing process is carried out withing 12 months from 1st January 2020. However, details of international filings and PCT filings and concepts of convention countries are discussed in the subsequent chapters to follow. Some gold standards associated with priority date are

- The invention can only be disclosed to the public after the priority date. Researchers can publish their research immediately only after obtaining a priority date
- Priority date is that cutoff date prior to which if any similar record in any form related to the filed patent application if obtained, could invalidate the said patent application during examination
- Patent granting is a long process which could take 3-5 years' time but when granted, patent protection starts from priority date which is the date of filing the patent application for the first time. Henceforth, once the patent is granted, legal action can be initiated against infringers if any suitable infringement evidence is found after the priority date. All evidences regarding to infringement of a particular patent application shall be entertained only if carried out after the priority date of the patent which has been infringed

3.3 Prior Art

Prior art comprises of all such information available in public domain which can be accessed either free of cost or on payment basis and is thought to have similarity to the invention being examined for grant of patent. In must be kept in mind that such information can be called as prior art only when those are available before the priority date as explained above. Prior art serves as legitimate evidences for establishing the novelty of an invention. Very closely similar prior art can be sufficient enough to invalidate a patent claim. Prior art can take the shape of,

- any published matter in any journal, magazine, book, newspaper or in any kind of print or electronic media. It also includes information available in any computer database system (collectively can be called as non-patent literature).
- patent literature – which indicates all patents documents filed in any country before the priority date of the invention being examined for grant of patent and deemed to be considered having relevance or similarity to the said invention under examination.
- any kind of practice being carried out by a community which has relevance to the invention claimed for patent.
- In other words, prior art for a particular invention is the available literature or knowledge (in practicable form) in public domain bearing resemblance with the said invention being examined for the grant of patent. However, information which is kept classified by the government doesn't constitute a prior art.

3.4 State of the Art

In case of any invention; the state of the art shall consist of all matter (either for a product or process) which before the priority date of that invention have been made available to the public by publication or by use anywhere in the world.

Example: if a patent is filed for the first time on 1st January 2021, then all matter related to the invention available in public domain throughout the world before 1st January 2021 (considered as the priority date) shall be considered to be a part of the state of the art.

Whatever disclosure related to a particular invention have taken place anywhere in the world in whatever language and to whatever extent of dissemination of the published matter; forms a part of the state of the art. However, such published disclosure should be directly available to the public for reference. Any classified (secret information) information shall not be a part of the state of the art. Sufficient care should be taken during inclusion of any available drawings in the state of the art. An available drawing may be considered as a part of the state of the art; if a skilled person can derive a technical teaching from them without further description or the available drawings sufficiently discloses the essential features of the invention being examined to such an extent that it can enable a skilled person to carry out the said invention or practice the said invention without undue requirement of further descriptions.

3.5 Person Skilled in the Art

This terminology is very frequently used in patenting system particularly when determining the inventive step (non-obviousness) which shall be discussed in the latter chapters to come. Such persons (or even group of persons in case of advanced technical area of invention) are those who are ordinary practioners in the art (said field to which the invention belongs) with such common knowledge at the relevant date (common knowledge existing in the said field before the priority date of an invention) which is generally thought to be possessed by an average person in the said field. Such persons even though in possession with everything belonging to the state of the art for a particular invention and capable of performing routine experimentation but still not able to work out the invention, the said invention is such situation is likely to be considered out of the thinking capability of a PSA. Some of the basic characteristics of a PSA are:

- possess only average knowledge
- lacks inventive capability
- aware of only routine experimentation procedures and shall not be able to perform complex experimentation
- afraid to try out new combinations and shall be conservative in approach
- lacks creative thinking and is likely to react with average thinking
- will arrive to a conclusion with average common-sense thinking

3.6 Anticipated Invention

According to the patent laws, anticipation of the invention means existence of any similar invention or disclosure of the said invention by any third party or the inventor himself in any form before the filing date of the patent application for a particular invention. To understand in simple words if any person(s) knew about the said invention or was using the said invention (product or process) before the patent application filing date then patent for the said invention cannot be granted as the invention is now said to be anticipated (further explanation given in chapter 5).

3.7 Applicant & Inventor

Applicant: An applicant is basically the owner of the patent. In the event of patent being granted, the exclusive patent rights will be vested on the applicant. Any revenue earned out of the commercialization of the patent will belong to the applicant. An applicant could be,

- the inventor himself
- the true/first inventor's assignee
- legal representative of any deceased true/first inventor or his assignee
- the employer of the inventor and was actually responsible for providing funding and infrastructure to the inventor(s) for carrying out the invention. Inventors in such case were working as employee of the applicant in lieu of salary.

An **Inventor** is actually a person or group of persons responsible for carrying out the invention. In the event of the inventor(s) filing the patent application in his own name, the inventor then also becomes the applicant. Thus, the inventor will be considered as the owner of the patent only when the patent application is filed in the name of the inventor.

Generally, when the inventor(s) have worked upon the invention on their own funding and doesn't represent any organization, then the patent application may be filed in the name of the inventor(s). However, if the inventor(s) belong to a particular organization such as a company or an educational institute or a startup and works as an employee in lieu of salary and if the said invention was funded by the organization then in such circumstances the patent application may be filed in the name of the organization, who then becomes the applicant. However, to exercise this cause, the concerned organization should have an active IPR policy which will dictate the rights and ownership of the inventor and the organization. Premier educational & research institutions such as CSIR & IIT's, NIT's etc. file patents for the inventions carried out by their faculties and research scholars in the name of the organization and also bears the cost of the patenting procedure. Same is the case with private companies. However, in the event of revenue being generated from the patent; a share of the same may be given to the inventors for their motivation, but that purely depends on the existing IPR policy of that particular organization. While filing an Indian patent in Form 1, the names of both applicants and inventors needs to be mentioned and the inventors declares assigning the rights to the applicant in the form of an endorsement if the names of the applicant and inventor differ.

3.8 Early Publication

When a patent application is filed for the grant of patent, the said application is published in the Indian patent office journal after 18 months. Prior to that, the application is strictly kept confidential and is not accessible to public. The application in digital format is stored in the server of the patent office for 18 months. Only after the publication of the patent application, it is available to the public for raising objection, if any. It is only after the publication has taken place, the application can be queued for the purpose of examination upon payment of prescribed fees and by filling up prescribed forms as request for examination. However, in-order to expedite the process of grant of patent, the publication of the patent application can be accelerated because the examination of the application by a patent examiner can begin only when the publication has taken place. So, by filing Form 9 and payment of additional fees apart from the standard filing fees, the publication can take place after 1 month of filing and subsequently can be taken up for examination {in accordance to Section 11-A(2), Rule 24-A}. This process of publication of the patent application after 1 month of filing is called as early publication (figure 3.2) which can be executed by filing Form 9 and payment of additional fees apart from the standard filing fee. However, it should be noted that such early publication can take place only when a patent has been filed with complete specification and for those applications which does not have involvement of secrecy issue (carried out when the invention has some relevance with defence system of India) as mention in Section 35,36,37,38, Rule 72 (concept of secrecy has been discussed in subsequent chapters to follow) However, there is no strategic advantage because the grant of patent (if granted at all) will be always from the date of filing the application. Early publication only speeds up the patenting process.

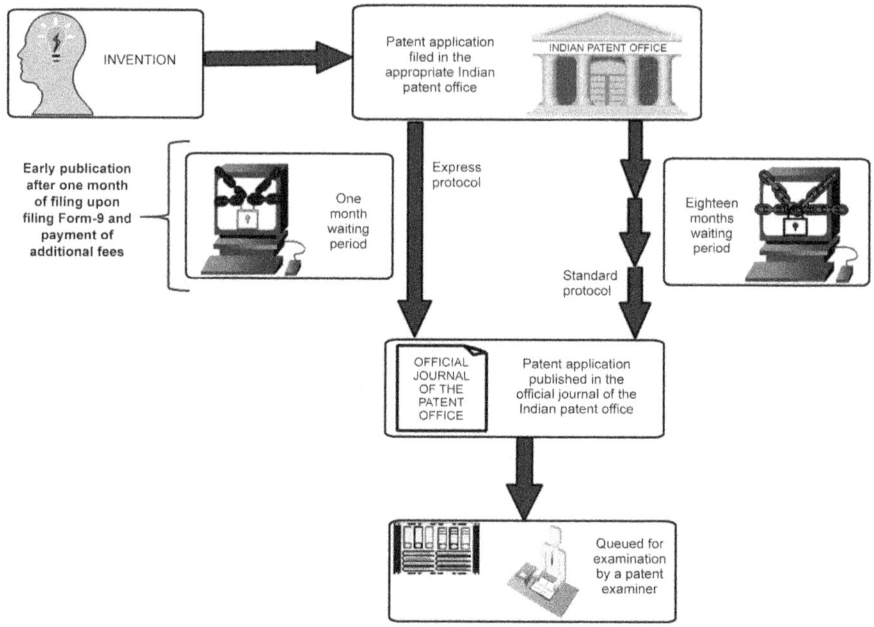

FIGURE 3.2 Illustrative explanation of early publication.

3.9 Post-dating

Post-dating indicates shifting of priority date of a patent application (either provisional or non-provisional) to a later date but not beyond six months from the actual date of filing the patent application under provision of Section 17 of Indian Patents Act. Such option of post-dating is not available in all countries like USA. Patent is a race with time, whoever files first is likely to get a patent. Having said this, no applicant who has filed a patent application would like to shift the priority date to a later date which may put the applicant in a backfoot in the race for patent. However, such post-dating may be required to meet the deadlines associated with the priority date. For example, if the applicant has missed the 12 months deadline of filing the PCT application from the priority date of filing the Indian application, the applicant in such case may post-date the basic Indian application so that the 12 months deadline can be extended as now the same deadline shall be calculated from the new date which was obtained through post-dating. However, there could be several such post filing formalities which needs to be performed in a time bound manner, where all such time line is calculated from the priority date. Nevertheless, post-dating can attract unnecessary trouble regarding novelty and inventive step. Because if a priority date is shifted to a later date (post-dating), then during the concerned period of post-dating, several new literature or disclosure may come up which may have taken place in the intervening period and can badly affect the novelty and inventive step of the application. Post-dating request for an application can be filed anytime before the grant of patent. In case such request is made before the examination of the application, then the examination time line shall be calculated from the new date obtained through post-dating. If such request is made after the generation of first examination report (FER), fresh examination now shall be conducted with time line calculated from the new date.

Example: If an original priority date of 1st January 2020 is post-dated to 1st May 2020 then such post filing formalities whose deadline is calculated from 1stJanuary 2020 shall now be calculated from 1stMay 2020 which may provide some relief in terms of meeting deadline for completing post filing formalities by the applicant. However, the applicant needs to understand that there could be lot of research or disclosures or patent literature coming up during the period of post-dating which in this case is 2nd January to 1st May 2020. Such disclosures cropping up during the post-dating period may even invalidate the patent application resulting in its rejection, which otherwise if not post-dated could have been accepted for grant of patent.

3.10 Compulsory Licensing

It is defined as grant of authorization by the Controller to a third party for using an already patented invention for commercialization without the consent of the patentee. Such licensing authority is directly granted by the Controller and shall not constitute a patent infringement. Any interested person can apply in Form-17 to the Controller requesting for compulsory license of a granted patent after expiry of three years from the grant of the said patent for which compulsory license is being requested. The reasons for applying for compulsory licensing are mentioned in Section 84 & 92 of Indian Patents Act which are as follows,

- if the invention has failed to meet the reasonable requirements of public – indicates that the commercial activities related to the said invention is harmfull to public, no proper demand or market opportunity for the patented invention has been created
- the patented invention is not available to the public at a reasonable price which a common man can afford - such aspect becomes important for those drugs which are very costly and can be afforded by only wealthier people or for life saving drugs which because of being patented are being charged at a very high price in India

- if the patented invention has not been made functional within the territory of India

The controller before taking any decision on the matter takes into account the following issues,

- nature of the invention and attempts made by the patentee for commercializing the said invention including attempts for licensing the same
- capability of the applicant demanding compulsory licensing to commercialize the said invention and make it available to the public and also whether the applicant can withstand the risk associated in commercializing the said invention
- conditions which lead to the inability of the patentee to commercialize the patented invention and making it available to the public at a reasonable price
- whether the applicant has made any prior attempts to seek licensing permission from the patentee

Upon receiving such request of grant of compulsory licensing for a patented invention, the Controller may ask the applicant to serve a notice to the patentee as well and shall publish such application in the official journal of the patent office. In case the patentee desires to oppose such grant of compulsory licensing, may file suitable opposition within two months from the date of publication in official journal. A copy of the opposition with necessary evidence shall also be sent to the applicant and notified to the Controller. The Controller shall study the written arguments of both the parties and may fix a hearing date and inform the parties at least ten days in advance. Depending upon the merit of the case, and taking into consideration the arguments, the Controller shall dispose of the matter by giving suitable decision. While granting the compulsory license (if any), the Controller shall secure the terms and conditions (according to the provision mentioned in Section 90 of Indian Patents Act) including the royalty or remuneration to be paid to the patentee by the licensee. Royalty or remuneration shall depend on the nature of the invention and the money invested by the patentee in the said invention to happen and other expenditures in getting the patent and maintaining the same. The Controller shall also ensure that the applicant is able to fully commercialize the invention predominantly in India (can export if required) and provide the end product to the public at an affordable price. Such compulsory license is a non-exclusive license which means that Government can further grant compulsory license for the same patented invention to other multiple vendors as the case may be. Central Government in case of a national emergency or any public health crisis situation (like the COVID-19 pandemic) at any time after the grant of patent, may order for grant of compulsory licensing to any suitable person so that the patented product could be made available to the public at an affordable price in such crisis situation or at situation of distress (Section 92 of Indian Patents act). Any interested person after such notification by the Central Government in the official gazette, may apply for accepting compulsory licensing of the said invention. Controller in such cases, ensures that the product reaches the public at the earliest and at the lowest price to overcome the crisis situation. Such cases particularly take place for patented pharmaceutical products or drugs. Patentee can apply for termination of compulsory license with suitable evidence (Section 94 of Indian Patents Act) in Form-21 once the patentee is of the opinion that the circumstances which lead to grant of compulsory license as mentioned in Section 84, no longer exists and such circumstances are unlikely to relapse. Such requisition from the patentee is however, open to contest by the holder of the license.

India's first compulsory license was granted to Hyderabad based firm NATCO for manufacturing & selling Bayer's 'Nexavar', a drug used in advanced stage of kidney cancer. The drug Nexavar was patented in India in 2008. On applying for compulsory licensing by NATCO, it was found that Nexavar could not be provided to common people in India at an affordable price. Moreover, it was also observed that Bayer had not manufactured or worked the said patent to a reasonable extent in India which was evident from the fact that Bayer was selling the drug in India at Rs 2.8 lakhs for a month's requirement of cancer therapy, whereas CIPLA was selling its version at Rs 28000 for a month's requirement of cancer therapy. In a landmark decision in 2012, India's first compulsory license was granted to NATCO who shall be selling the said drug at Rs 8880 for a month's requirement of cancer therapy and it was further ordered that NATCO shall be paying a royalty of 6% over its net sales of the said drug.

CHAPTER 4

Indian Patent Office

The Office of the Controller General of Patents, Designs and Trade Marks (CGPDTM) is a subordinate office functioning under the Department of Industrial Policy and Promotion, Ministry of Commerce and Industry. Executives of the rank of Joint secretary from the said Ministry exercises administrative and supervisory control over the office of CGPDTM (including geographical Indications). The Controller General administers the working of the Patents Act, 1970, the Trade Marks Act, 1999, the Geographical Indications of Goods (Registration and Protection) Act, 1999 and the Designs Act, 2000 and also renders advise to the Government on matters relating to Intellectual Property Rights. The Office of the CGPDTM is located at Mumbai. Four Patent Offices are situated in India (Delhi Office, Mumbai Office, Kolkata Office and Chennai Office) with Kolkata being considered as the Head Office. As per the Indian Patents Act, 1970 the Controller General is treated and addressed as the Controller of Patents who administers the Indian patent system. The act also provides provision for the constitution of an Appellate Board to admit and handle appeals arising out of the orders of the Controller of Patents. The Controller is the overall competent authority of the four Patent Offices. The appointed patent examiners as per the provision of the Patents Act and other officers of the Patent Office discharge their administrative functions under the direction of the Controller. The hierarchy of the officers at the Patent Office is presented below for easy understanding.

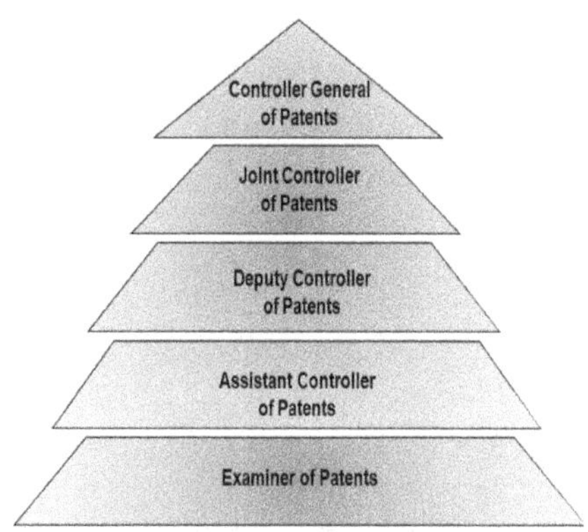

FIGURE 4.1 Hierarchy of the officers at the Patent Office.

The CGPDTM delegates his powers to Senior Joint Controller of Patents & Designs, Joint Controllers of Patents & Designs, Deputy Controllers of Patents & Designs and Assistant Controllers of Patents & Designs regarding various procedures for patent grant. The CGPDTM is the authorized signatory for all issued patent certificates. The organisational structure of CGPDTM is depicted in Figure 4.2.

The four patent offices of India have been assigned territorial jurisdiction for executing all the official procedures related to patent examination and grant. The first applicants address which is recorded in FORM 1 actually decides in which patent office the application should be filed. This point is very important if there are joint applicants as in that case the filing jurisdiction will be decided by the address of the first applicant. The address could be place of residence or business or address of the organization or the place where actually the invention took place. The below mentioned table 4.1 indicates the jurisdiction covered by the four patent offices of India along with their address.

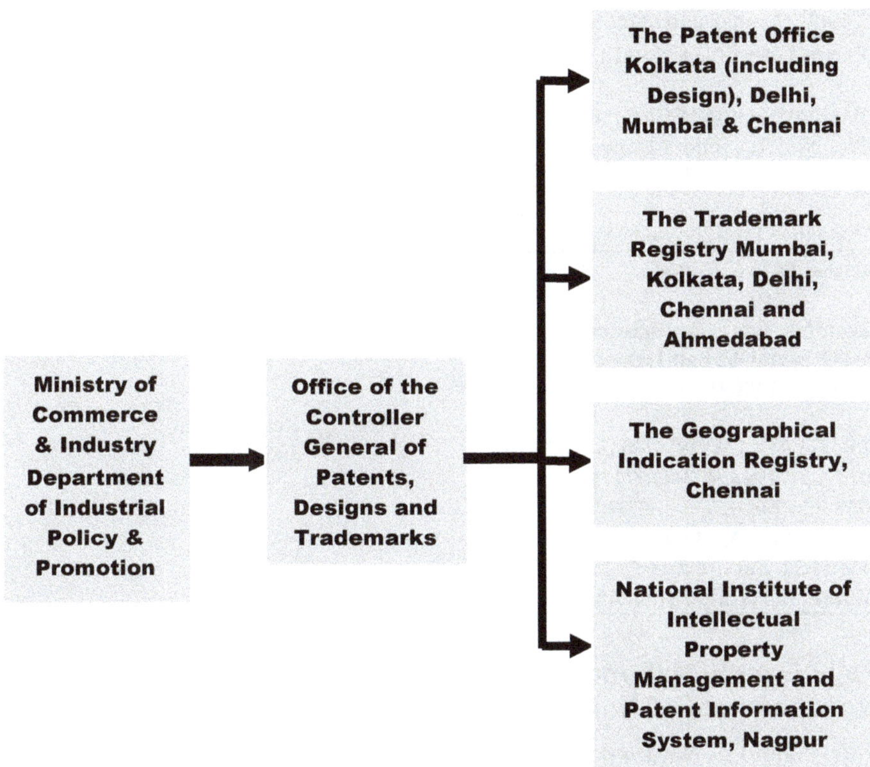

FIGURE 4.2 Organisational structure of CGPDTM.

TABLE 4.1 List of patent offices in India along with their territorial jurisdiction.

Office	Territorial Jurisdiction
Patent Office, Mumbai **Boudhik Sampada Bhavan,** **Antop Hill, S.M. Road,** **Mumbai-400037** **Phone: 022-24132735** **Email: cgoffice-mh@nic.in**	Maharashtra, Gujarat, Madhya Pradesh, Goa and Chhattisgarh and the Union Territories of Daman and Diu & Dadra and Nagar Haveli
Patent Office, Chennai **Patent Office Intellectual Property Building** **G.S.T. Road, Guindy,** **Chennai-600032** **Phone: 044-22505242** **Fax: 044-22502066** **Email: chennai-patent@nic.in**	Andhra Pradesh, Karnataka, Kerala, Tamil Nadu, Telangana and the Union Territories of Pondicherry and Lakshadweep
Patent Office, New Delhi **Boudhik Sampada Bhawan,** **Plot No. 32, Sector 14, Dwarka,** **New Delhi-110078** **Phone: +91-11-25300207**	Haryana, Himachal Pradesh, Punjab, Rajasthan, Uttar Pradesh, Utarakhand, Delhi and the Union Territory of Chandigarh, Jammu and Kashmir and Ladakh.
Patent Office, Kolkata **Boudhik Sampada Bhawan,** **CP-2 Sector V, Salt Lake City,** **Kolkata-700091** **Phone: 033-23671987, 033-23679101, 033-23671943, 033-23671945, 033-23675090, 033-23675093, 033-23676685, 033-23677320** **Fax: 033-23671988** **Email: kolkata-patent@nic.in**	Rest of India.

Rajiv Gandhi National Institute for Intellectual Property Management (RGNIIPM)

Rajiv Gandhi National Institute for Intellectual Property Management situated at Nagpur is a Central Government Institute functioning as a dedicated center for excellence in capacity building in the field of Intellectual Property Rights that is in line with the global norms and also safeguarding the national interests simultaneously (email: rgniipm.ipo@nic.in). The institute functions under **CGPDTM** and basically caters to the need of training newly appointed patent examiners and also other IP professionals on various aspects of IPR. It also imparts basic education and awareness on IPR to the community as well. The institute exclusively undertakes preparation of study reports and policy analysis on behalf of the Government. The institute building was inaugurated on 21st July, 2012 by the then Hon'ble Union Minister of Commerce & Industry and Textiles. The basic mandate of the organization is to facilitate development, creation, use and exploitation of Intellectual Property and working of Intellectual Property system.

The institute conducts a number of training programmes on IPR considering the requirements of the potential users. The beneficiaries are business & law professionals, IPR agents, R&D organization personnel's, entrepreneurs, University faculties, Government officials and individual interested persons. Apart from the exhaustive training given to the newly appointed patent examiners which generally continues for a month, short term training programmes ranging from 1-6 days on various IPR relates issues are organized for beneficiaries as mentioned above. The training programme can be attended by booking a seat in advance on payment of prescribed fees which depends on the number of days of training. Fees could be approximately INR 10,000 for a five-day training programme. Accommodation assistance with food arrangement is provided by the organization on additional payment. The institute also jointly conducts workshops and awareness programmes on IPR with other educational institutions on payment basis (Rs 10000 – 25000 depending on the structure of the workshop and number of days involved for a limited number of participants). In this COVID pandemic situation the institute is frequently conducting webinars which can be attended on payment basis. The details of every training schedule are posted on the website (https://ipindia.gov.in/rgniipm.htm) on regular basis.

The Patent Information System (PIS) which operates in the same building of RGNIIPM was set up by Government of India in 1980 with the aim to develop a data center/data bank consisting of comprehensive collection of patent literature on worldwide basis to fulfill the information requirements of various organizations involved in R&D. The PIS provides the following services:

1. Services related to patent search
    - *State of Art Search*: provides bibliographic data and abstract of patent document related to a particular invention as requested by the user

- *Bibliographic search*: provides only bibliographic data of patent documents
- *English equivalent patent search*: English language equivalent patents for patents in languages other than English
- *Patent family search*: bibliographic details of a family member of a patent are provided
- *Assisted search*: access to databases, journals and other information sources subscribed by the PIS

2. *Patent copy supply service*: maintains the full text of all patent documents from India as well as those from foreign countries, copies of which can be obtained on payment basis.

Some of the good administrative practices of the Indian patent office are:

(a) Comprehensive e-filing facility which is available 24×7 with more than 70 banks involved in the payment gateway. Applicants can own a personal space in the cyber environment of the patent office.

(b) Paper free office, where electronic processing of all patent application is undertaken through strategically designed modules which are assigned separately to applicants, patent examiners and Controller

(c) E-generation of patent certificate which is available directly on the website

(d) Realtime status of the application can be seen in the website after publication, with all files related to the application place in one platform

(e) Free public search facility

(f) QR coded office communication

(g) Specialized committed examiners group for evaluating various types of application like evaluating inventions related to traditional knowledge and pharmaceuticals

(h) Capacity building and awareness programmes on IPR being conducted by RGNIIPM

(i) Indian Patent Office is also designated as one of the International Search Authority (ISA) for PCT application

CHAPTER 5

Patentable Subject Matter

5.1 Novelty

For the purpose of grant of patent, the said invention must fulfill three basic litmus test which are as follows,

- The product or process claimed for patent should be novel and should have an inventive step (means the invention should be non-obvious)
- The product or process claimed for patent should have industrial application
- The product or process claimed for invention should not attract any provisions mentioned in Section 3 of Indian Patents Act which describes those inventions which are non-patentable

It is of extreme importance to keep the novelty of the invention intact which means no information related to the invention for which patent is expected to be filed should leak out in the public domain in any form. It should be kept in mind that the subject matter of the invention should not form a part of the state of the art. Loss of novelty will result in weakening of the patent claim for the particular invention and even can result in patent rejection. The following general principles are applied by the examiner during evaluation of the filed patent application in accordance with the provisions mention in Section 13, read together along with the provisions mentioned in Section 29-34 of the Indian Patents Act. If an invention gets anticipated before the filing of the said invention (priority date), the novelty is deemed to be considered as "lost". The invention for which patent is being claimed must be different from all available published articles, known techniques and any known commercial product already in use in the public domain anywhere in the world. According to the patent laws, anticipation of the inventions means existence of any similar invention or disclosure of the said invention by any third party or the inventor himself in any form before the filing date of the patent application for a particular invention. To understand in simple words, if any person(s) knew about the said invention or was using the said invention (product or process) before the patent application filing date, then patent for the said invention cannot be granted as the invention is now said to be anticipated. Described below are the following conditions in which an invention is considered to have been anticipated and thus results in loss of novelty:

- If anything, similar to the said invention have been filed for patent in India or in any country before the priority date of the said invention which is being evaluated for grant of patent
- If anything, similar to the said invention is already available as published literature (both patent and non-patent literature) in any language and in any form anywhere in the world
- In case of prior claiming (Section 13(1) b of Indian Patents Act): if any of the claims mentioned in the complete specification of the said invention whose novelty is being ascertained, forms the subject matter of any distinct claim(s) for an earlier published patent application with complete specification in India on or after 1st January 1912, before the priority date of the filed invention and published after the filing of the said invention which is being examined. For establishing prior claiming, only those Indian patent applications filed with complete specifications prior to the filing date of the said invention whose novelty is being ascertained are only considered
- If the said invention (product or process) is already in use in public domain
- If the said invention forms a part of the knowledge (oral or otherwise) available within any indigenous/ethnic community in India or anywhere in the world.

Thus, anticipation is considered as a parameter for judging the novelty of the said invention and based on the above-mentioned principles the novelty can be either maintained or invalidated.

5.1.1 Determination of Novelty

The patent examiner to whom the application is allotted carries out the novelty test as a part of the patent office protocol. In this process the patent examiner determines if the invention which is being examined for the grant of patent can be anticipated by prior publication (patent and non-patent literature) anywhere in the world, by prior claim available in any published Indian patent (filed before and published after the filing of the invention under examination) and by use of the said invention in any indigenous/ethnic community anywhere in the world. This is the "absolute NOVELTY" concept that is followed by India and many other countries for patenting. Novelty is determined prior to inventive step because it becomes very important to understand the original creative contributions that is being reflected from the said invention which can be understood only in the light of the novel elements involved in the invention. In order to demonstrate lack of novelty, the obtained disclosure (prior art) which can likely destroy the novelty of the invention which is being examined, should be entirely composed as a single document which means that the disclosure should be capable of reflecting every element of the invention which is under examination. However, it doesn't mean that only one disclosure can be cited for invalidating the novelty but multiple documents if cited, then each should stand on its own, if the novelty of the said invention is going to be attacked. Scrapping and collecting information from multiple disclosures and presenting a cumulative report is not allowed for invalidating the novelty of any invention. Cumulating the teachings or information available in multiple disclosures for destroying the novelty is known as mosaicing which is strictly prohibited in the process of determining novelty but allowed while determining the inventive step which will be discussed in the latter part of the chapter.

Once the possible similar disclosures related to the filed invention are obtained by the patent examiner, he has to use his common general knowledge to determine how closely are the information mentioned in the obtained disclosure similar to the filed invention. Since there is no computer software or technology to derive the similarity index between the disclosures and the filed inventions, it depends purely on the understanding of the patent examiner which definitely can be challenged by the applicant if the decision does not go in favour of the applicant. In some cases, the claimed invention may not fully match with the earlier available disclosures (eg. patent literature), but still the novelty of the claimed invention can be invalidated if the patent examiner finds that there are only minor differences between the two (available disclosure and claimed invention).The basic principle used by the examiner is that the obtained disclosure should have sufficient disclosed information or teachings so that it enables a person skilled in the art to carry out the invention or practice the said invention without undue burden of complex experimentation. In short, if the disclosures completely enable a person skilled in the art to carry out the invention then the prior art or disclosures obtained can be considered close enough to invalidate the novelty of the filed application. The invention also lacks novelty if any prior disclosure or information obtained thus falls within the scope of the said invention (invention for which patent is claimed). In simpler words, it means that if the claimed invention mentions any alternatives or range of values (like composition of an herbal mixture or formulation, temperature range etc.) and if any of the alternatives or any value within the range provided happens to form a part of the prior disclosure already available, then the novelty is considered to be neutralized. In light of the above fact, it can further be stated that a specific disclosure destroys the novelty of a generic feature mentioned in the claim which has been filed but the reverse may not be true. This means a generic feature shall not deprive a specific claim from novelty.

Example: disclosure of copper (specific example/disclosure) neutralizes the novelty of metal (generic example) but not the novelty of any other metal except copper

While determining novelty following aspects are also taken into consideration

- Language of prior art (any disclosure similar to the invention filed for patent) is not a limitation. Disclosures obtained in any language is acceptable
- All kinds of text books, journals, newspapers, magazines are considered regardless their circulation status or number of copies sold.
- Degree of dissemination of any prior art is not a limitation. It is not considered that how many people have actually seen the concerned prior art or disclosure if available in the public domain. If the matter is available in public domain it is enough to invalidate the novelty test
- Any communication (written document) made to the government in relation to a particular invention cannot be treated as a disclosure for attacking the novelty of a filed invention. As such communications to the government even if seen by few people in the government system of working are not disclosed to the common public and rather kept confidential or treated in a classified manner. Since such information cannot be inspected by public so they do not form a part of the state of the art for neutralizing novelty claim of any invention.

5.2 Not Anticipations (Section 29-34)

According to the patent laws, anticipation of the invention means existence of any similar invention or disclosure of the said invention by any third party or the inventor himself, in any form before the filing date of the patent application for a particular invention. The constitution of anticipation for a particular patent application which ultimately destroys the novelty of the invention is different for different countries. There are certain circumstances mentioned in Indian Patents Act (Section 29-34), occurrence of which shall not make the invention claimed deemed to have been anticipated and hence its novelty survives. **A one-year grace period** is provided as per Indian Patents Act and also by some other countries (USA), in such circumstances occurrence of which; will not destroy the novelty. But the patent application has to be filed within one year of occurrence of such circumstances as mentioned below. Below mentioned are those circumstances, which if occurs will not form a ground for breach of novelty for the filed invention,

(i) ***Prior Publication (Section 29)***: any disclosure of an invention to the public before the priority date or filing date of the application will not be deemed as anticipated, if the patentee or the applicant proves that the publication (in any form whether as patent literature or non-patent literature) was published without the knowledge of all the applicants involved or some of the applicants were in darkness regarding such publication either in any journal, newspaper or magazine of any country. If the patent application is filed immediately upon learning about the above-mentioned incident and within one year of appearance of such publication in the public domain, the invention will not be anticipated and the novelty persists. However, the onus of proving that publication took place without the consent of all the involved applicants lies on the applicants themselves. Section 29 also states that any invention shall not loose its novelty, if the same was published in any patent application filed in India before 1st January 1912. However, it should be kept in mind that if any invention has been commercially practiced with the consent of the inventor before the filing of patent application, Section 29 shall not hold true in such case and as a result novelty will be destroyed.

(ii) ***Previous communication to Government (Section 30)***: If the invention has been communicated to the government or to any person authorised by the government before the filing of patent application, then such communication shall not constitute anticipating of invention which could have resulted in breach of novelty otherwise. If the inventor communicates the invention to the government for any purpose like examination of the invention, or may be seeking financial support or any other purpose and in the due process few people in the government machinery comes to know about the invention through an official channel, such act would not then cause breach of novelty.

(iii) ***Prior public display***: If the inventor displays his invention in an exhibition (notified by the central government) and also as a consequence the invention gets published in some brochure or leaflet of the said exhibition, the invention will not be deemed to be anticipated if the patent application is filed withing 12 months from the opening day of such an exhibition. The provision is still applicable if some unauthorized person other than the inventor displays the said invention in such an exhibition.

If the inventor or some person with the consent of the inventor reads out or presents the invention as poster presentation or oral presentation before a learned society in some seminar or conference, the invention will not be deemed to be anticipated if the patent application is filed within 12 months of occurrence of such incident.

(iv) ***Prior Public Display (Section 32)***: If the nature of the invention is such that reasonable trial of the invention cannot be conducted within the four walls of the laboratory like a road making machine, then such trials as per the requirement of the invention can be carried out in open which is visible and accessible to public. Such public display for the purpose of carrying out reasonable trials regarding the invention shall not constitute an anticipation if the patent application is filed within 12 months from the date of conducting such prior public working.

(v) ***Anticipation by use and publication after provisional specification (sec 33)***: If the invention has been used and published after filing a provisional application, then a complete specification filed shall not be deemed to have been anticipated.

However, it should be kept in mind that disclosures related to the invention for which patent filing has not been done should be refrained or avoided. However, if such disclosures happen out of ignorance, this particular grace period of one year is provided by Indian Patents Act which can still protect the novelty of the invention provided necessary action is taken within the grace period given.

5.3 Inventive Step (Non-Obviousness)

Once the Novelty has been established, the next test conducted by the patent examiner is determination of inventive step (non-obviousness). These are all subjective tests based on the expert understanding of the examiner in light of the available prior art. The golden principle in this regard is that if an invention appears obvious to a person skilled in the art with the existing knowledge available on the priority date, the invention is deemed to be considered as lacking an inventive step according to the provision mentioned in Section 2(1) (ja) of the India Patents Act. The purpose behind ascertaining the inventive step is to understand the technological advancement that has taken place in that particular invention from the known existing knowledge in that field. In other words, inventive step for a particular invention estimates the magnitude of the technological improvement that has taken place over the available prior art. If enough evidences are obtained which clearly signifies the quantum of technological improvement then the invention is considered to be meritorious and thus deserves to be patented. On the other hand, those inventions which just reflects mere workshop arrangement and rearrangement indicates simple extension of available prior art and thus becomes obvious to a person skilled in the art. Thus, inventive step clearly distinguishes a meritorious invention from a mere workshop arrangement type invention. It should be borne in mind that the size or volume of the invention does not play any role in making it a meritorious invention but the intellectual intent involved in that invention is estimated. The above statement can be understood in light of the below mentioned illustrative example,

Example: An applicant Mr. X files a patent application in the field "I" having invented a device by combining parts A1 and A2. If any person skilled in the art of "I" or practicing "I", gets motivated with his routine thinking capacity to try and see what happens by combining A1 and A2, and thus arrives to the said invention in the field of "I", then the invention becomes obvious, lacking inventive step. Because in such case any ordinarily skilled person in "I" can think of combining A1 and A2 to reach to the present invention. So, such invention which can be easily thought of or derived using basic logical thinking, lacks inventive step.

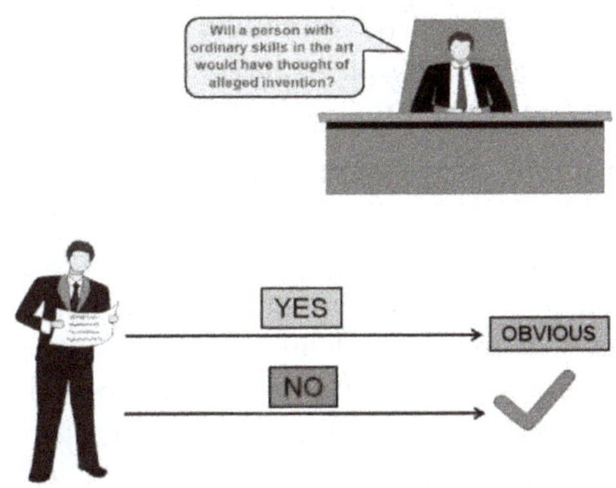

The final judgement regarding inventive step is taken by the examiner by trying to find out a judicious answer to the question – whether the person with ordinary skills in the art would have thought of the said invention using his common general knowledge? If the person skilled in the art is of the view that he would not have arrived at the invention or rather thought of the invention using his routine normal thinking and routine skills, then it indicates that the inventor has made significant technological contributions and the invention has enough merit to be considered as meritorious. If the person skilled in the art is of the view that he would have easily thought of the invention using his routine common-sense knowledge, then the invention becomes obvious and is deemed to be considered lacking an inventive step.

An obvious invention can be thought by any person skilled in the art as it is just a simple extension of the already existing knowledge. The term "obvious" reflects something very common which does not go beyond the routine progress but follows a common sense and logical thinking pathway. Some of the ideal characteristics of being obvious are

- Not thinking differently, rather following traditional thinking pattern

- Arriving to something based on simple logical thinking
- Exercising routine skills, lack of creative thinking
- Not willing to try out new combinations to solve a particular issue

In simpler words, if any invention can be thought of with logical sense then the quantum of technological improvement is very poor indicating lack of inventive step. When an invention possesses an inventive step, then that particular invention was beyond the normal thinking of a person skilled in the art.

While determining inventive step, unlike novelty, mosaicing of documents is permitted. If an invention can be produced by combining the teachings from different published literature available before the filing of the patent application, then the invention is considered to be obvious to a person skilled in the art and thus inventive step is destroyed. In simpler words, let's assume that three documents (D1, D2, D3) are found having similarity with the invention under examination (filed for grant of patent). If by combining the teachings available from these documents, any person skilled in the art can arrive to the said invention using logical understanding then it clearly reflects that the said invention is just a piece of extension of the already existing knowledge and cannot be considered meritorious enough to have an inventive step. The invention as a whole must be considered while assessing the inventive step.

Example: component A and component B have specific functions and are not dependent on each other for their working. Now, if an invention is made by combining component A & B, then by combining the teachings available from component A and B, any person skilled in the art can easily using logical understanding can come to the conclusion that the invention comprising both these components will have an aggregation of the features of both the components.

Inventive step becomes a critical issue for those inventions which comprises of mixing various components or parts. If an invention comprises of mere superimposition of some parts, then the invention is very likely to be obvious as the product would then comprise of aggregation of properties of the parts involved. If an invention tries to verify previous predictions but does not add anything which can be cited as a significant advancement, inventive step is considered to be lacking. When from a number of possible alternatives one can be chosen to arrive to a particular invention, inventive step is considered to be lacking. When an invention just provides equivalents or substitution to the already known knowledge, inventive step is understood to be missing. If an invention makes new use of an already known material, inventive step is said to be missing. While determining the inventive step, the following points are taken into consideration,

- Scope and content of the prior art for a particular invention
- Assessment of the technical results and economic significance (economic success) of the claimed invention
- Understanding the differences between the relevant prior art and the invention under examination
- Understanding the technical problem that is expected to be resolved by the said invention
- Finally, non-obviousness is decided based on the fact that whether a person skilled in the art could bridge the differences between the existing prior art and the invention under examination. If the differences could be bridged by the person skilled in the art then inventive step is deemed to be lacking.

The following provides conclusive evidence of existence of inventive step (non-obviousness) in an invention

(i) *Distance*: If there is enough evidence to conclude that there is a huge technological gap between the prior existing knowledge and the current invention which is being investigated, inventive step can be established.

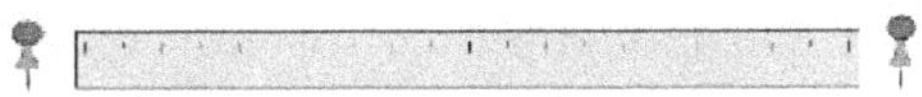

(ii) *Surprising Effect*: This is important particularly when an invention comprises of combination of several parts or mixing of several ingredients. A routine mixing only produces an aggregation or cumulative effect of the individual components. Such invention lacks inventive step but if a surprising effect can be exhibited arising out of such mixing or combination which was beyond the normal imagination of a person skilled in the art, inventive step is established.

(iii) *Long Felt Need*: If it is understood from the present invention that it successfully solves a long-felt requirement, inventive step is established. As there was a long felt need so many inventors might have tried the same but could not succeed. Such inventions cannot be fulfilled through routine logical thinking and with routine experimentation otherwise there would not have been a long felt need and somebody might have invented it long before a need could have been really felt.

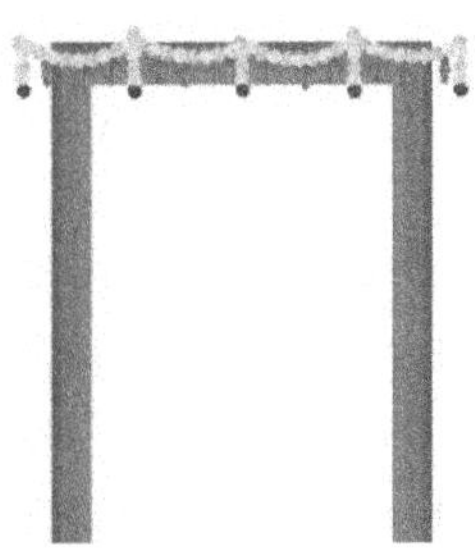

(iv) *Failure of Others*: If a particular invention indicates solving a problem which was attempted by many researchers in the past but could not achieve success, inventive step is said to be established. Since many researchers did attempt to solve the problem but without any success, so it clearly indicates that the problem could not have been solved by routine thinking or by routine experimental skills, otherwise there would not have been failures. The inventor who succeeded must have done something different which is beyond the normal thinking of a person with ordinary skills, hence the invention can be considered meritorious for a patent.

(v) *Complexity of Work*: If the work performed by the inventor to arrive to the particular invention was complex and beyond the capacity of a person skilled in the art to achieve the invention with routine experimental skills, inventive step is said to be established. Such complex work requires unconventional thinking and the inventor has to try out different combinations which cannot be thought by a person with ordinary skills, hence such inventions cannot be obvious.

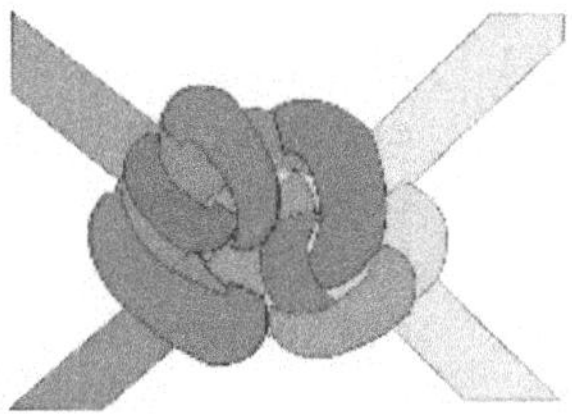

(vi) *Commercial Success*: If an instant invention fulfills a commercial need or creates a commercial success may be by creating an invention which is likely to decrease the cost of the already existing product and make it affordable for a common man, inventive step may be thought to be present (indicative but not conclusive).

Case Study on Inventive Step

The famous landmark court case of Hindustan Metal Industries (plaintiff) vs. Biswanath Prasad RadheyShyam has set new lessons on inventive step. Hindustan Metal industries who initiated the legal proceedings is a registered partnership firm involved in making of brass and German silver utensils at Mirzapur. Biswanath Prasad happens to be also involved in the same business as a separate person based in the same town.

Hindustan Metal Industries patented a method in 1951of utensil making which is more safe, fast, efficient and produces utensils with better finishing. The patentee came to know that another person named Biswanath Prasad RadheyShyam was using the patented invention for production of utensils without any authorization, hence, the patentee filed an infringement case which was countered by Biswanath Prasad with a revocation plea on the ground of lack of novelty and inventive step. The Allahabad High Court observed that the said invention is just a mere workshop arrangement and rearrangement of a traditional method which has been in practice since several decades before the filing of the said patent. Hence, any such invention which was already in practice lacks novelty and the said invention was also found to lack inventive step as well, thus the patent was revoked by High Court. The judgment became a landmark decision and new teaching on inventive step was provided by the High Court,

- The fundamental principle behind granting a patent is that it should be new and useful to the public. The invention should be the original discovery of the inventor himself and not just a verification of what was already known before filing of the patent.
- When the invention is regarding an improvement, it should be able to produce new, better and cheaper article than before and the improvements or combinations invented should be independently able to pass the test for inventive step and should reflect something beyond a mere workshop arrangement.

5.4 Industrial Application

An invention must have some defined practical usage and cannot be absolutely theoretical. The following conditions must be satisfied for the invention to be considered industrially applicable. The invention,

1. Can be made
2. Can be used at least in one field of activity
3. Can be reproduced with the same characteristics as many times as necessary.

To be patentable, an invention must be useful, but mere usefulness is not sufficient to support the patentability of a patent application. Utility is not determined by the element of commercial or pecuniary success and has to be determined with reference to the state of things at the filing date of the patent application. For example, suppose the invention was usefull at the time of patent filing but subsequent technological advancements in due course of time made the said invention obsolete and commercially nonviable, this fact however, is not sufficient to neutralize the patent from utility point of view. Speculations regarding industrial use are not accepted.

5.5 Not Patentable Inventions

Section 3 and 4 of the Indian Patents Act specifies certain types of inventions which cannot be patented. However, the below list is just an illustration which indicates certain types of inventions and is not conclusive in nature. Every invention filed for patent is judged individually on its own merit.

Different clauses indicated in Section 3 (a-p)

(a) Any invention frivolous in nature, which mean inventions which are of no important use, lacking usage sense and not worthy at all or those inventions which are against the well-established natural law cannot be patented. Natural law in this case means if any invention is against laws of gravity or laws of motion etc.

Example: A clock with 20 hours of time display with each one hour divided into 90 minutes. This is a frivolous invention and also against the well-established pattern of time keeping. Such inventions serve no specific purpose or worth and is likely to cause confusion. Any machine which is claimed to give 100% efficiency or can produce output without any input requirements falls under the category of inventions against the natural law as there could be no machine which does not require an input for providing output.

FIGURE 5.1 Illustrations of frivolous invention.

(b) Any invention whose primary use could go against public order/morality or the use is likely to cause some serious danger to the life of human, animals, plants or may even damage the environment.

Example: any device used for committing theft/burglary very easily, a gambling machine, machine for printing fake currency, process for food adulteration, cloning methods for humans as it is against moral values.

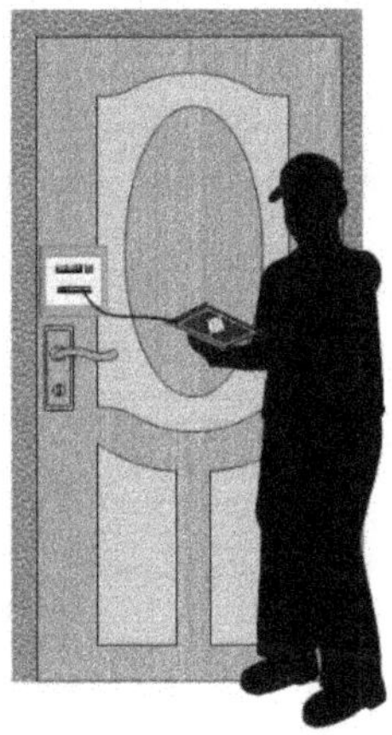

FIGURE 5.2 Illustration of an invention (a device for breaking a lock) which is against public order/morality and also involves risk to human life.

(c) Discovery of any kind of scientific theory/principle or formulation of a sort of abstract/theory or discovering any living or non-living substances occurring in nature.

Example: A scientific theory or an abstract theory is a statement about the natural world and hence cannot be patented but using such theory or principle, if any process or product is developed, then such product or process could be patentable subjected to requirements of novelty and inventive step. Henceforth, all the scientific theories and principles like, Newton's laws of motions, Einstein's theory of relativity, Archimedes' principles etc. are manifestations of nature and is available to all and hence they were not patented. Any mineral which was not known to mankind if discovered from nature, any new microorganism isolated from environmental sample or discovered from nature by mankind also cannot be patented as per the above principle. It should be kept in mind that these are mere discoveries and any sort of discovery cannot be patented as all these substances were already existing in nature and were just found out. Patent is always applicable to "inventions" which never existed before but was created for the first time. Patent is not associated with "discovery" as "discovery" signifies prior presence of the substance before being known to all.

(d) Discovery of any new form of an already known substance but with no enhancement in the efficacy from the previously known substance. Discovery of any new use or property of an already known substance or use of known process or product or machine for a different purpose other than the already known is not patentable.

Example: repurposing of drugs (ivermectin, hydroxychloroquine, vitamin C etc.) for treatment of other diseases cannot be patented. In the COVID-19 pandemic we have seen that several already known drugs were repurposed for the treatment and management of COVID-19, since all these drugs were already known for a specific use and might have been patented for their first use reported hence, cannot be patented once again if a new use is suddenly discovered.

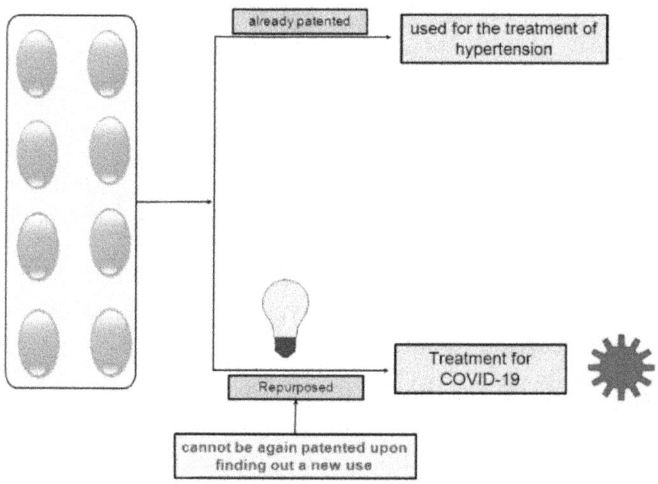

FIGURE 5.3 Illustration representing that discovery of a new use of an already known substance is not patentable.

Similarly, in pharmaceutical research if a new derivative (inclusive of salts, esters, isomers, complexes and other types of derivatives) is made from an already known parent molecule, then the derivative is considered to be the same as that of the parent molecule unless, proven to differ drastically in term of efficacy. So as far as pharmaceuticals are considered, the factor of proving drastic improvement in properties related to the efficacy of the derivative is a conclusive factor in granting of patent.

(e) Any substance which is produced by simple admixture which results in cumulative effect of the properties of the individual components involved in the admixture, or a process of producing such admixtures cannot be patented.

Examples: If component A and component B are mixed together to form a new product, then the said product will just display the cumulative properties of both the components involved. In order to make such product patentable, exhibition of tremendous synergistic effect (surprisingly more than just aggregation of individual properties) is required. Such synergistic effects should be clearly mentioned in the description of the invention by means of comparison.

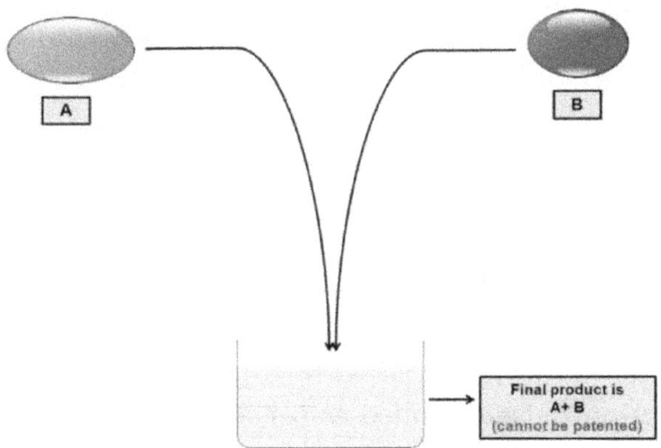

FIGURE 5.4 Illustration representing that any substance produced by mixing two substances whereby the final product represents the cumulative effects of the properties of the two mixed substances, is not patentable.

(f) Arrangement or re-arrangement or any kind of duplication of known devices each functioning independently in a known way is not an invention.

Examples: if two devices functioning independently are juxtaposed or placed one after another, does not yield a new product and hence is not patentable. In order to make it patentable, the cited improvement over what is already known should appear far better than just a workshop arrangement and should yield a new product where each of the juxtaposed components should be capable of passing the test for novelty and inventive step separately. Such juxtapositioning of components which functions independently (not meritorious enough to be patented) include torch attached to an umbrella or LED lights attached to an umbrella, fan attached with an umbrella, torch attached with a bucket etc.

FIGURE 5.5 Illustration representing that two independently functioning components if juxtaposed does not constitute a new invention which can be patented.

(g) Clause (g) now stand omitted as per the 2002 amendments made in the Indian Patents Act and the omission is effective from 25.05.2003

(h) A method of agriculture or horticulture is not patentable

Examples: a method of producing a plant even by altering its natural growth conditions, method of mushroom and algae production and a method of soil production from soil with nematodes by treating the soil with specified phosphorathioates are not patentable.

(i) Any process dealing with medicinal, surgical, curative, prophylactic, diagnostic, therapeutic or other treatment of human beings or any process for a similar treatment of animals to render them free of disease or to increase their economic value or that of their products is not an invention.

Example: As per the above provision, the below mentioned categories cannot be patented

- Medical methods: method of administering a drug through any route (oral, injectable, patch etc.)
- Surgical methods: an art of making surgical cut with minimal bleeding, art of making of stitch free cut or cataract removal etc.
- Treatment methods: treatment of malignant tumor cells, method of removal of dental plaque
- Prophylactic treatment: art of administering vaccines

- Diagnostic methods: art of diagnosing a disease by speculations made from studying specific symptoms or body reactions

However, if any apparatus or device is invented which can be used for surgical therapeutic or diagnostic purpose can definitely be patented subjected to passing of test for novelty and inventive step.

(j) Plants and animals in whole or any part thereof other than micro-organisms but including seeds, varieties and species and essentially biological processes for production or propagation of plants and animals are not inventions. The following are kept outside the scope of patentability,

- Whole or part of any plant
- Whole or part of any animal
- Species of plants and animals
- Biological methods involved in the propagation of plants and animals
- Microorganisms which are available from nature. However, genetically modified microorganisms are patentable

(k) A mathematical or business method or a computer programme per se or algorithms are not inventions and hence not patentable.

Example: An act of performing mathematical calculations (like multiplications, square roots etc.) or developing strategic business models are all mental exercises and hence cannot be patented. Algorithm are specific instructions written in computer readable language and stored inside a computer memory and can be read and executed by a computer only. Such matter is considered as a part of software and hence not patentable in India. However, if the same software is used to run a device or machine then the hardware effect which the software produces can be patented.

A new mathematical model for book keeping, a business model for keeping accounts is all result of mental act and hence cannot be patented

(l) A literary, dramatic, musical or artistic work or any other aesthetic creation whatsoever including cinematographic works and television productions is not an invention

Explanation: various types of literature related works, electronic databases, drama, choreographic works, photographic & cinematographic works, sculpture, architecture, music etc. are not patentable and can be protected under copyright.

(m) A mere scheme or rule or method of performing mental act or method of playing game is not an invention and hence not patentable.

Explanation: a method of playing chess or any kind of game, different methods of teaching, method of operating a machine etc. are not patentable.

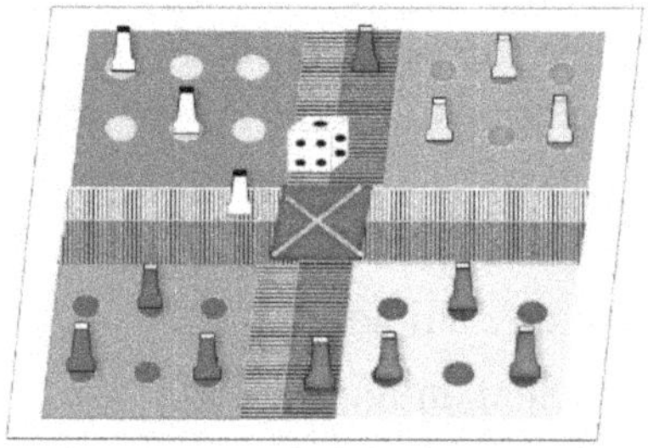

FIGURE 5.6 A method for playing a game is not patentable.

(n) Presentation of information

Explanation: An art of expressing an information in a unique way with the help of audio-visual facility cannot be patented.

FIGURE 5.7 Illustration representing that mere art of presenting any information cannot be patented.

(o) Topography of Integrated Circuits

Explanation: The protection of Layout Designs of Integrated Circuits is regulated separately under a different act called the Semiconductor Integrated Circuit Lay-out Designs Act, 2000 which provides provision for protection of three-dimensional configuration of the electronic circuits used in microchips and semiconductor chips. Henceforth, patent is not granted for such invention but a separate protection system in the form of above-mentioned act is available.

(p) An invention which in effect, is traditional knowledge or which is an aggregation or duplication of known properties of traditionally known component or components is not an invention

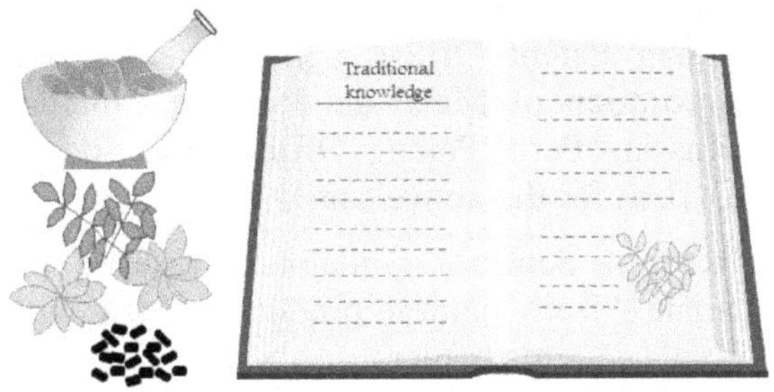

FIGURE 5.8 Any invention which is a part of traditional knowledge cannot be patented

Explanation: The medicinal action of different medicinal plants available in nature cannot be patented (like wound healing properties of turmeric, antibacterial property of neem etc.). Such medicinal property are a gift of nature and inherent quality of that particular plant and is not subjected to invention. Moreover, such traditional knowledge exists in the public domain as a common basic household knowledge which is passed from one generation to another and have been in practice since ancient times. Earlier there have been cases where patent was granted by other countries on uses of turmeric (healing properties) and neem (fungicidal properties) which were then subsequently revoked after suitable defence from India. It was Dr. R.A.Mashelkar whose exhaustive efforts led to revocation (rejection) of such patents. Such incidents let to a hard felt need to develop a system for keeping vigilance related to such patents being filed anywhere in the world. In this regard the cumulative efforts of Banaras Hindu University, Gujrat Ayurvedic University, National Institute of Ayurveda-Jaipur and Central Council for Research in Ayurveda and Siddha (CCRAS)-Delhi, led to the development of an indigenously compiled digital database known as the Traditional Knowledge Digital Library (TKDL - http://www.tkdl.res.in/) containing information of more than 2 lakh traditional formulation prepared from medicinal plants and currently available in five international languages, namely, English, Japanese, French, German and Spanish. The formulations mentioned in the TKDL database are considered to be public property. Indian government has entered into agreement with patent offices of other countries that TKDL database will be searched for finding any prior art for any patent filed which has relevance with traditional knowledge. Currently TKDL database is available to the patent offices of thirteen countries (European Patent Office, United State Patent & Trademark Office, Japan Patent Office, United Kingdom Patent Office, Canadian Intellectual Property Office, German Patent Office, Intellectual Property Australia, Indian Patent Office, Chile Patent Office, Intellectual Property Corporation of Malaysia, Rospatent-Intellectual Property Office of Russia, Peru Patent Office and Spanish Patent and Trademark Office) for the above said purpose.

However, there are separate guidelines available for patenting of inventions arising from natural products which will be discussed separately in subsequent chapters.

Section 4

As per the provision mentioned in Section 4, patents cannot be granted for any invention which is related to atomic energy as described in Section 20(1) of the Atomic Energy Act, 1962. Even any substance (updated list of such substances as notified by the central government and is available at www.dae.nic.in) which may be used for the production or use of atomic energy or any research related to atomic energy cannot be also patented. If any such patent application is submitted which has relevance with atomic energy, then the said invention is referred to the Central Government by the Controller for clearance. The Central Government upon considering the matter provides necessary directions regarding the disposal of the concerned application. The decision of the Central Government in this regard is final which cannot be challenged.

CHAPTER 6

Patent Types

Based on the nature of the patent specification, patents can be **classified as provisional and complete specification (application)**. Specification in patents refers to a techno-legal document containing all necessary disclosures regarding the invention for which the patent has been filed. Disclosures must comprise of all scientific and technical information required for performing the invention in the best possible way, presented in such a descriptive manner that a person with ordinary skill in the art (belonging to the same field to which the invention relates) can perform or practice the invention without undue burden of experimentation. Specification is the heart of a patent application and forms the basis for\ claiming patent rights based on the "claims" mentioned in the specifications.

6.1 Provisional Patent Application (Section 9)

If the applicant is of the opinion that the invention has achieved a stage when it can be disclosed in a presentable form (in terms of patent filing and not to public) but has not yet attained conclusive outcome or completeness of the invention has not been attained so far, under such circumstances the applicant can still file a provisional patent application. This provision is of great help in securing a priority date when the applicant knows that there could be many other inventors working on the similar area. If many patent applications are filed on similar invention, then the patent actually is granted (subjected to fulfillment of all norms such as novelty and inventive step) to the applicant who files first, irrespective of the country of filing. Henceforth, when the invention is close to completion (not yet completed) and ready for partial disclosure, provisional patent application can be filed. Once provisional application is filed, the applicant gets 12 months' time to complete the invention and later file with complete specification within 12 months. If the applicant successfully files a complete specification within 12 months of filing of the provisional application then the priority date is considered from the date of filing provisional application which means that the priority date is preserved. Let's us understand the concept with the help of an illustrative example,

Example: Company A, B and C all are working on the same invention (consider an anti-tuberculosis drug). Company A thinks that they are almost close to attaining the invention of the drug and was aware of the provisional application system. The filing dates of all the three companies are mentioned below

Company A - files provisional application on 1st January 2020. Company A after filing provisional application completes the invention and subsequently files complete ordinary application with all specifications on 1st November 2020 which is well within the 12 months grace period.

Company B - waits for completion of the invention and files complete specification (complete ordinary application) on 1stJuly 2020 (considered as priority date for Company B)

Company C - also waits until the completion of the invention and files complete ordinary application on 1st August 2020 (considered as priority date for Company C)

It should be kept in mind that patent application is examined for grant of patent only when complete specifications are filed. No examination for grant of patent is conducted based on provisional filing. Having said this, it is clear from the above example that Company A was the last to file a complete specification on 1st November 2020. But since Company A had already filed a provisional specification on 1st January 2020, so automatically it gets 12 months grace time to file a complete specification (ordinary application) for consideration of patent grant. Since company A has taken necessary action in the given grace period so its priority date will be preserved and even though the complete specifications were filed on 1st November, 2020, still the priority date shall be given as the date of filing provisional application which is 1st January 2020. As a result, Company A gains an advantage over priority date from the other companies. If the above case, the invention which is similar in nature made by all the three companies even though meritorious enough, Company A is only eligible for patent because of an earlier priority date whereas Company B & C is likely to lose the test for novelty and non-obviousness because of a later priority date.

While filing provisional application "claims" are not mentioned as the invention is not yet thought to be completed. Claims reflect the patent rights which is actually granted and should be mandatorily present in a complete specification filed for an ordinary application. All other disclosure such as title, descriptions like field of invention, background, object and statement of the invention and drawings (if any) which are an integral part of Form-2 should be described. Different Forms and their contents which are required at the time of filing patent application shall be discussed in subsequent chapters separately. Form-2 which is a mandatory form for filing patent application should contain maximum information as much as possible except the "claims" in case of provisional application. This is done to ensure the exact nature of invention mentioned in the provisional application, because if within the period of 12 months a new element of invention suddenly crops up which was not indicated in the provisional application, then that new invention which had come up during the grace period and was mentioned later during filing of the complete specification will not be entertained for obtaining the priority date advantage of provisional filing. In such case, the new element of invention which has suddenly cropped up has to be filed as a separate application with no benefit of earlier provisional filing and as a result such application which bears the new element of invention will have a separate fresh date (priority date). If the applicant files multiple provisional applications and if the Controller is of the opinion that all these separately filed provisional applications reflects the same type of invention, the Controller in that case may ask the applicant to file only one single complete specification (ordinary patent application) within the given grace period. In such case, the date of filing of the first provisional application (out of the multiple provisional applications filed by the same applicant) will be considered as the priority date upon filing the complete specification. As per Section 9 of the Indian Patents Act, the applicant may also request the Controller to convert a complete specification filed as ordinary patent application into a provisional application within 12 months of filing the complete specification. In that case the applicant has to then submit again complete specification within the grace period given.

Advantages of provisional application

- Priority date is preserved for 12 months from the date of filing the provisional patent application. If within the given grace period, the applicant files complete specification in the form of ordinary patent application, the priority date is restored which means the date of filing of the provisional application is considered as the priority date in case of filing complete specification (ordinary patent application) as mentioned above through an illustrative example
- Grace period of 12 months from the date of filing the provisional application allows the applicant to complete the invention and draft the complete specifications meticulously
- Cost of filing provisional application is less when compared to filing complete ordinary application. Within the given grace period the applicant gets enough time to arrange for extra revenue needed for further filing and other procedures

- From the date of filing provisional patent application, the applicant can use the term "patent pending" for his particular invention which shall safeguard his invention from potential infringers. If the applicant files the complete specifications within the given grace period and in due course of time if the patent is granted, then the patent protection shall be awarded from the date of provisional filing which shall be considered as the priority date since the applicant has taken necessary action within the grace period. Henceforth, till the patent decision is obtained the applicant can proceed with the commercialization of the invention in a manner as if the patent has been granted and hence can use the term "patent pending". Any possible invading action to the said invention by competitors during the pendency period shall be considered as potential infringements if the patent gets granted later on. However, if the patent is not granted then such intrusions cannot be considered as infringements and the invention can now be used by anybody.

6.2 Complete Specification (Ordinary Patent Application, Section 10)

It is techno-legal document containing the complete description of the invention with "claims" mentioned based on which patent rights can be claimed. Such application has to be filed only when the applicant is of the opinion that the invention is complete or can be filed either within 12 months, if provisional application regarding the said invention has been filed earlier. The following are the ideal characteristics of complete specification (ordinary patent application)

- Should fully describe the invention disclosing the best mode of performing the invention so that it can enable a person with ordinary skills in the art to carry out the invention without any undue burden of unknown experiments.
- The application should end with "claim(s)" defining the scope of the invention for which patent right is being claimed
- If any biological material is involved, proper reference regarding depositing the same with the designated International Depository Authority should be made (discussed in detail in subsequent chapters)
- Must disclose the source of such biological material
- Must contain an abstract
- Should contain specific references as the case may be if there is any association with divisional application or patent of addition.

Provisional patent application	Complete ordinary patent application
Invention at this stage is not yet 100% complete	Invention is 100% complete
"claims" are not mentioned in the specification filed	"claims" needs to be mandatorily mentioned
Filing fee is less	Filing fee is more
12 months' time period is given after provisional filing in-order to submit the complete specification	This is the final version of the patent application and no amendments are possible unless asked by the Controller after generation of first examination report
Abstract is not required	Abstract is mandatory
Provisional application cannot be automatically converted to complete specification as the later needs to be filed separately within 12 months of filing of provisional application	Complete specification within 12 months of filing may be converted to provisional specification upon request by the applicant
Provisional application status is lost, if complete specification is not filed within the grace period of 12 months	The status of complete specification remains valid unless the patent application is rejected by the controller post examination or if examination fee is not paid within the prescribed time limit after publication of the application (discussed in later chapters)

6.3 Divisional Application (Section 16 of Indian Patents Act)

The provision of divisional application is explained in Section 16 of the Indian Patents Act. The word divisional indicates dividing or splitting the parent patent application into multiple applications. Divisional patent application is filed when claims mentioned in the complete specification (ordinary patent application) is indicative of the involvement of more than one invention or group of inventions which are not connected by a single inventive concept or there is reflection of more than one inventive concept from the claims, then Indian Patents Act provides a remedy in the form of divisional application. Such application may be filed by the applicant anytime before the grant of patent when the applicant so desires or when asked by the Controller based on the objections related to multiple inventions being reflected from the claims raised during generation of first examination report.

Key points to remember in case of divisional application:

- Divisional application gets a separate existence status and hence is given a separate application number but the same filing date as that of the parent application.

  Example: An applicant files an ordinary patent application on 1st January 2020. The applicant on realizing the involvement of multiple inventions in the claims mentioned, files a divisional application on 1st June 2021. In this case the divisional application will get a separate application number but the filing date (priority date) of the divisional application will be treated as 1st January 2020.

The independent existence of the divisional application indicates that following activities have to be done separately treating divisional application as a fresh application

- Separate fee needs to be paid
- Separate request for examination needs to be filed
- Separately prosecuted
- Gives rise to an independent patent but the said patent will expire with the patent obtained from the parent application

- The priority date of parent application and any later filed divisional application are same
- Divisional application(s) are examined with regard to the parent application
- Claims of divisional application are obtained by separating the claims from the parent application. No new claims can be added which were not mentioned in the earlier parent application
- The divisional application has to be filed in the same patent office where the first parent application was submitted
- The complete specification submitted for the divisional application must contain a reference to the original parent application, splitting of which has given birth to divisional application.
- All the fees associated with a patent application have to be paid for the divisional application as well
- If the original patent application was handled by a patent agent to whom the Power of Attorney was transferred by the applicant by filing Form 26, the same need not be done again for a divisional application and the earlier Form 26 shall sustain
- Proof of right (Form 1) since filed at the time of the parent application may not be submitted again in case of filing of divisional application

6.4 Patent of Addition (Section 54)

If the applicant is of the opinion that an improvement or some modification has occurred from the already filed invention or for which a patent has already been granted, the applicant than in that case may apply for a patent of addition. Improvements and modifications are natural ongoing process and is expected to happen anytime. Such improvements can take place in pursuit of improving an already available invention or based on the feedback received from the end users after commerciallization of the invention. Patent of addition provides an excellent opportunity through which such modifications and improvements can be protected. Many countries have abolished the system of patent of addition but some countries still practices it such as India, USA, Australia etc.

Key points to remember in case of patent of addition:

- Application for patent of addition can be filed both before as well as after the grant of the main patent application over which certain improvements are claimed through patent of addition
- Patent of addition can only be granted when the main application for patent has been granted
- Patent of addition is possible when the applicants in the main application and in application filed for patent of addition are same
- While filing patent of addition, reference of the main application should always be given stating that the application so filed consists of improvements and modifications of an earlier filed patent application or earlier granted patent
- If an applicant is in possession of two separate patents where the subject matter of one patent is a sought of improvement or modification from the other patent, then the Controller may convert one of the independent patents into a patent of addition. However, the applicants in both the patents should be same in-order to exercise this provision
- The date on which patent of addition is actually filed, is considered as the date of filing for the said patent of addition application
- Patent of addition has the same life span as that of the main patent and expires with it. In case the main patent gets revoked due to opposition or any other reason, the patent of addition will not loose its existence and shall continue as an independent patent
- Separate renewal fee for maintaining the patent of addition is not required
- Patent of addition cannot be revoked specifically on the basis that the modification or improvements claimed in the patent of addition does not involve an inventive step with regard to the main application

6.5 Convention Application (Section 133)

Patent is a territorial right. An invention which is patented in India will be protected in India only. Competitors outside India can manufacture the same or use the same as long as such activities are carried outside India without constituting infringement issues. The only solution to this problem is by applying for patent registration in foreign countries as well and one convenient mode of doing so is by filing convention application. Convention countries are those which are a signatory to any international, regional or bi-lateral treaty. The treaty referred to here is the Paris Convention of 1883. The provision under convention application allows an individual to make international patent applications in those convention countries which are signatory to the Paris Convention based on prior patent filing (basic application) made in any of the convention countries without losing the priority date if filed within 12 months from the filing of basic application. Thus, an applicant can secure his invention in multiple countries without losing the priority date obtained from the basic application, if necessary filing action is taken within the given time frame. Let us understand the concept with the help of the below example and in light of the fact that India is a signatory to the Paris convention since 1998.

Example: Consider an applicant has filed an Indian patent on 1st January 2020. Considering the fact that his invention is likely to be used in multiple countries, the applicant files the same invention for patent registration in multiple countries (all convention countries – member of Paris Convention) on different dates after 1st January, 2020, but within 12 months from the date of filing in India (1st January 2020). In this case the first application filed in India will be known as basic application and since the application was filed in convention countries within 12 months from 1st January 2020, so the priority date of all international applications made in multiple convention countries will be considered as 1stJanuary 2020 which happens to be the filing date of basic application. Moreover, all the foreign countries where the application was filed will treat the application as if it was their own national application filed by their own country people. Such provision offers great advantage to applicants for protecting their invention in multiple countries without actually losing the priority date advantage obtained by virtue of filing the basic application. Also, the period of twelve months allows sufficient time to the applicant to decide which countries to choose for international filing and also to arrange for revenue to incur the cost of foreign filing.

Key points to remember in case of Convention Application:

- In case two separate patent applications have been filed in more than one convention countries and if the invention relates to the same inventive concept, it is still possible to combine both of them and file a combined single patent application in respect of already disclosed specifications in the basic application, in any convention country if done within 12 months.
- Every convention application must be accompanied with a complete set of specification and abstract as well.

- The date of filing of the basic application must be specified. A certified copy of the priority document (document which mentions the filing date of the basic application) may be required in English language.

6.6 International Application under PCT (Section 39)

Patent Cooperation Treaty (PCT) is an international agreement entered upon by more than 150 countries who are members of Paris Convention. The treaty (PCT) came into existence in 1970. The treaty allows an applicant to file an international patent application in multiple countries with priority date advantage by filing just one common international application. There is no term called international patent which will provide protection of the invention all-round the globe. The invention has to be protected in multiple countries as desired by the applicant by separately applying in different countries according to the patent rules of that particular country. Such a job becomes a difficult process which further becomes complicated due to complex paper work involved in the filing process which has to be in accordance with the rules and requirements of that particular country. In order to simplify the process so that an applicant can seek protection in all contracting states of PCT (countries who have agreed to enter into PCT agreement) through just one international application, the concept of PCT international filing was evolved. The process of applying for PCT international application is explained in detail in a later chapter. Thus, as far as international patent filing is considered, two common modes are present – convention application and PCT international application. It may be noted that PCT norms are valid only among the member countries. Let us understand the process through an illustrative process as explained below,

Example: An Indian applicant files an Indian patent application. The applicant now wishes to file patent application in multiple countries (like the United State of America, Australia, UK) for the protection of his invention. In normal circumstances the applicant has to study the patent rules of each country and carry out the filing procedures as per the paper requirements of every countries patent office. Under such circumstances, date of filing in every country is likely to differ. International filing under PCT allows the applicant to file just one common patent application at the designated international office and if the applicant does so within 12 months of filing the national application, the priority date is protected when filed in subsequent contracting states.

Date of filing Indian patent application: 1st January 2020

Date of filing of PCT international application: 1st October 2020

Conclusion: through the PCT common international application the patent application will enter into all contracting states under PCT as indicated by the applicant during filing. Since the PCT international application was filed within twelve months of 1st January 2020, so the priority date of the application in all PCT countries (as selected by the applicant) will be considered as 1st January 2020.

Key points to remember in case of PCT International Application:

- All international applications under PCT are treated by the member states as if it is their national application filed by a citizen of their own country
- A grace period of 12 months is obtained after filing national application to decide on international filing without losing the priority date of the national filing. Within this time period the applicant can manage his revenues required for the expenditure of international filing and carry out market research also at the same time.
- Prior permission from Indian patent office is required before international filing. After the completion of the international filing and after a time period of 30/31 months from the priority date, the PCT application enters the national phase of the PCT member countries (contracting states). During PCT international filing the applicant has to choose among the member states where the application has to enter as national phase. Once the application enters the national phase of the chosen country after the expiry of 30/31 months from priority date, the applicant has to pay the fees applicable as per the rule of each member country and also have to produce a certified translation of the basic application according to the acceptable language of that particular country's patent office. The decision whether the patent will be granted or not depends on the patent rules of that particular country as patent rules differs from country to country.

CHAPTER 7

Patent Filing Steps

The previous few chapters have so far discussed the basic understanding behind patent and patenting. Having said this, innovation is no doubt a creative original product of human intellect but at the same time it is equally important to understand that protecting the said invention in the form of a patent is also not an easy task. A lot of paper work, thorough knowledge of patentable subject matter, procedures involved in patenting and defending the application during examination are also required and plays a key role in getting the patent granted. Below mentioned is an overview indicating the step-by-step procedure involved in the process of filing a patent application in India and subsequent process thereof leading to the grant or rejection of the patent. The details of every step have been taken up one by one for exhaustive explanation in the next chapter.

1. ***Filing of Application***: Several Forms have to be filled up before actually filing the patent application. Out of them, the minimum requirement is Form 1 and Form 2 which is mandatorily required for completing the filing process. Sufficient time even after submission of application is provided to the applicant for submission of other mandatory Forms. The filing of the patent application can be done through either by physical filing or e-filing (most desirable). Paper filing is a traditional process whereby, the applicant after filling the details required in all the mandatory Forms, submits them to the appropriate patent office either through postal service or depositing the same at the respective patent office counter. Electronic filing is a computerized filing procedure carried out from previously registered account and is guided by the filing software very similar to any online exam registration process. The chances of committing an operational/procedural error while operating through e-filing mode is unlikely to happen as the filing software is extremely comprehensive in nature and the software guides the applicant in filling up all

mandatory entries required initially for a successful patent application submission. The different Forms are already structured in the submission portal and the applicant just needs to fill the entries which are being asked in the prescribed space. The supporting documents like drawings, abstract, complete specification, other minor Forms etc. needs to be uploaded by the applicant. Other details regarding the application can be filled up in the appropriate dialogue box appearing in the software. All Forms submitted through e-filing mode have to be digitally signed using digital signature. The necessary fees associated with the filing process which needs to be paid at the initial stage can be submitted through online payment option during e-filing whereas, in case of physical filing the same can be deposited either through bank demand draft or cash at the designated cash counter of the patent office. The total fees are automatically calculated by the software based on the forms being chosen for submission. Electronic filing or digital filing is highly encouraged as the process can be completed at the comfort of one's own place and the process is guided by the software where chances of making a mistake in the filing process is highly unlikely

2. ***Processing of Application***: At this stage detailed examination of the patent application is not done rather some preliminary checks are carried out to ascertain that the submitted application is in order as required by the patent office. However, if the application is submitted by e-filing mode, the system itself auto-generates the application number and the documents are already available in digital form and in prescribed format and order. Nevertheless, if the application has been submitted through physical filing mode, the applicant may commit some mistakes and thus preliminary checks and issuance of application number needs to be done. The patent office also checks if the application has been filed at the appropriate patent office or not? and whether the submitted patent application has any relevance with atomic energy or not, because if any relevance is obtained the course of the said application shall take a different route (described in the later chapter). There are four patent offices in India and different states are located under the jurisdiction of respective patent offices. It is very important to ascertain that the applicant had filed the patent application based on the applicable jurisdiction at the appropriate patent office. The factors determining the jurisdiction of the applicant are discussed in the next chapter. At this stage it is also important to

ascertain that the filed application also has no relevance with atomic energy, otherwise, as per the provision of Section 4 of Indian Patents Act (described in previous chapter) patent cannot be granted on such inventions.

3. ***Publication of Patent Application*:** After filing of patent application, the concerned application in digital form is stored in the server of Indian patent office for a normal course of 18 months. For this time period of 18 months, the application cannot be traced using the application number by general public and neither any reference of the application can be obtained from the patent database available online to the public. The application is stored confidentially in the server of the Indian patent office with limited access to some selected designated officers of the patent office. However, this lock period of 18 months can be shortened to one month by filing Form 9 (early publication). If done so, then the application which was supposed to be published after 18 months as standard protocol, now will get published after one month as a consequence to filing Form 9. Once published, the application now can be traced by searching the Indian patent database using the application number. The reference of the same can be obtained through internet search as well by any public. Publication takes place in the official journal of the Indian patent office which is published on weekly basis on every Friday. The journal can be downloaded free of cost from the Indian patent office website (https://ipindia.gov.in/journal-patents.htm). Publication doesn't mean that the entire application with all specifications is published in the journal, instead some basic information along with the abstract is published which is explained in the next chapter. Nevertheless, once the application is published, all documents submitted along with the application at the time of filing are uploaded on the patent website which can be viewed by general public. At this stage the invention is still protected, and upon reading the available documents, if somebody attempts to copy the invention and use it commercially will still qualify for attracting infringement consequences once the patent gets granted. However, as soon as the application is published, the period of pre-grant opposition begins where any person can file a pre-grant opposition in prescribed format anytime before the grant of patent (discussed in detail later in the opposition and revocation chapter).

4. ***Examination of patent application*:** Once the patent application gets published after the normal course of 18 months or after 1 month (based on filing of Form 9), the application then can be considered for examination. However, the application will be queued up for examination only when request for examination is filed in Form 18 with prescribed fees. If the request for examination is not filed within 48 months from the priority date, the application is considered to be withdrawn by the applicant. So, basically examination of patent application begins only when the application is published and when request for examination is filed in Form 18 with necessary fee. Based on the subject matter of the invention and area of specialization of the examiner, the application is allotted to a suitable examiner located at any four patent offices of India. The process is a paper free job and the respective patent application is uploaded by the Controller into the module of the respective examiner for the purpose of examination. The outcome of the examination is the First Examination Report (FER) which issued to the applicant or to his authorized agent as the case may be.

5. ***Reply to FER*:** The issued FER will contain several objections related to novelty, inventive step and non-patentability aspects as mentioned in Section 3 of Indian Patents Act. In light of the objections raised, the examiner may ask the applicant to amend the application or the claims mentioned. A suitable clarification and necessary amendments (if any) have to be furnished by the applicant or by his authorized patent agent in the prescribed time. Any kind of filed pre-grant opposition is also taken up during the examination of the application and forwarded to the applicant for providing suitable justification or clarification. If after studying the filed clarifications, the examiner feels that conclusive evidence has been provided which are good enough, the examiner may waive all the objections and may declare the patent to be in order for grant. Nevertheless, if the examiner is not fully satisfied with the clarifications or the amendments filed, the examiner may ask the applicant or his authorized patent agent to attend a hearing through video-conferencing to present the arguments verbally (hearing through video-conferencing is subjected to payment of fees by the applicant). Upon hearing the applicant or his authorized agent, the patent application may be declared to be found in order for grant or may be rejected based on the merit of the case. In this regard, the

merits of the pre-grant opposition are also considered and if found good enough, can form a basis for rejection of patent application. If the invention has any involvement of medicinal plants, necessary approval from National Biodiversity Authority, Chennai has to be obtained separately and submitted to the patent office. In such cases only after obtaining the said approval, the patent will be finally granted. All the updates associated with the progress of the application is posted in the website under the page of the respective application and an intimation email is also send to the email registered during the registration process for creating an account for the e-filing submission.

6. ***Grant of patent*:** If the Controller is of the opinion that the patent application does not contravene any of the provisions mentioned in Indian Patents Act, or the application cannot be refused by virtue of the power vested to the Controller, the patent will be granted by the Controller. The date of grant is actually the date on which the patent gets the grant status but the patent protection will be from the date of filing the patent application for a period of 20 years. The Indian patent office follows an electronic processing system and hence status of grant is immediately reflected in the website under the page of that particular application. The patent certificate bearing a particular serial number is generated electronically in the prescribed format and is entered in the Register of Patents on the date of grant itself. All these processes are completed electronically. However, even after the grant of patent, post-grant opposition is open for a period of one year from the date of notification of grant in patent office journal (discussed in detail in later chapter). In order to keep the patent active, renewal fees need to be paid till the expiry of the patent, else the patent will lapse.

A schematic flowchart (figure 7.1) depicting the different procedural steps involved in patent application processing is given below for easy understanding of the readers,

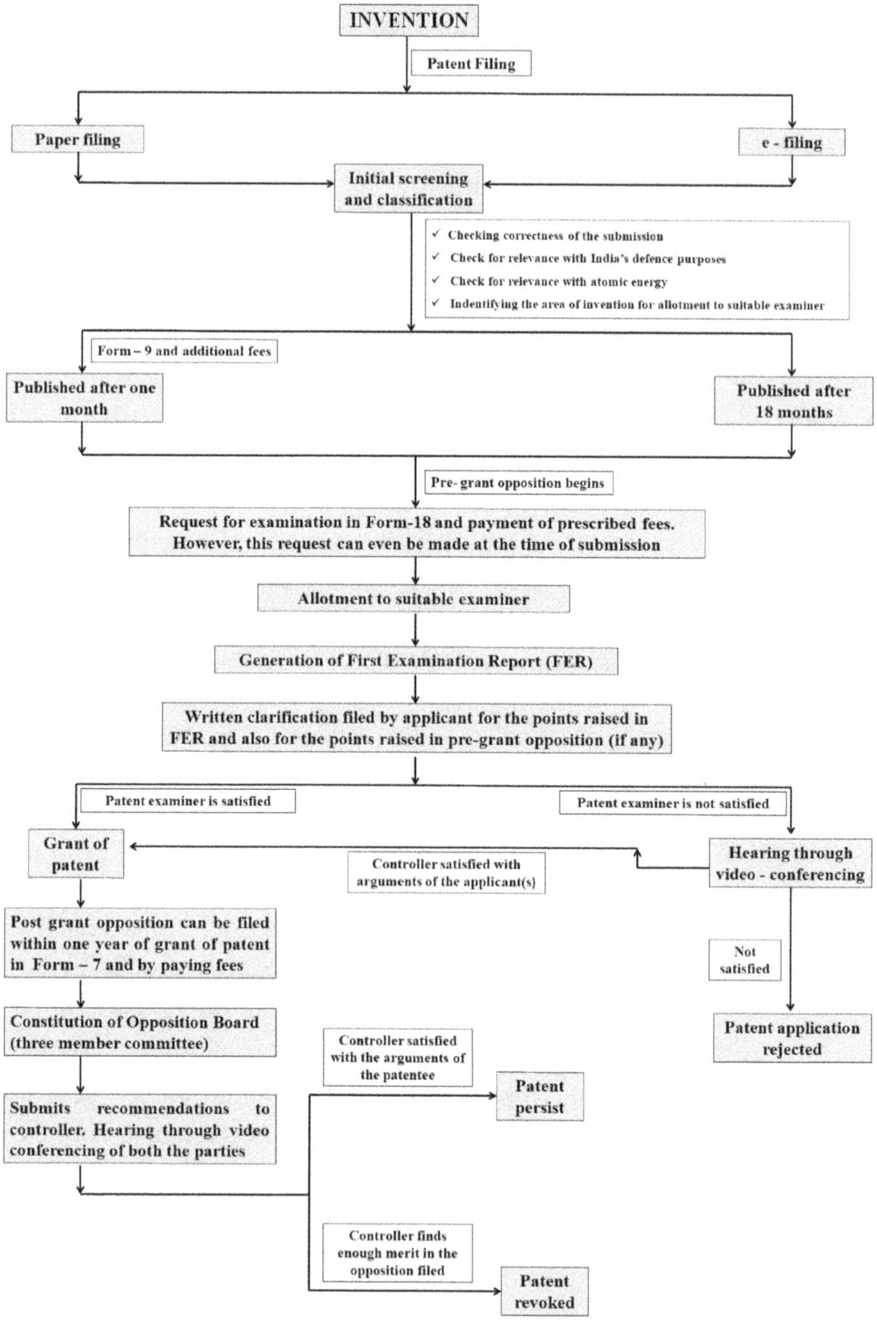

FIGURE 7.1 A schematic flowchart depicting the different steps involved in patent application processing starting from submission of application to disposal of the application.

CHAPTER 8

Patent Drafting and Application Processing

8.1 Document Handling and Drafting

It is very important to understand the paper work involved in getting the patent application good enough ready for filing. This particular chapter shall deal with the documents involved during initial filing of the application and other documents required during the course of patent application processing. Nevertheless, preparing various documents for the filing process becomes easy to handle if e-filing is carried out which is a computer software guided process. Commonly used Forms are available as drop-down options and the details asked can be directly filled up through the software. The software then consolidates the filled information and automatically generates the desired form, in such case the applicant need not worry about the exact format. However, filling up the requisite forms in prescribed format becomes critical when the applicant chooses paper filing where all documents are prepared manually and then submitted through postal service or in person at the respective patent office counter. This chapter shall deal with the requirements of various mandatory Forms/documents required to complete a successful patent application filing.

The two basic Forms that are required initially at the time of filing are Form- 1 and Form- 2. Form- 3 and Form- 5 are also mandatory but sufficient time even after filing the application is provided for submission of Form- 3 & 5, which means their submission is not mandatory at the time of filing. Below are described various Forms and documents required for successful filing of an ordinary Indian patent application.

8.1.1 Form-1

This Form is the basic patent application form. An application for the grant of patent for a particular invention is thus made in Form- 1 by any of the following persons either alone or jointly

- True and first inventor (does not include any person who first imported the invention in India)
- True and first inventor's assignee
- Legal representative of deceased true and first inventor

Once the necessary information is filled up in the prescribed allotted space of Form- 1 as shown in the software, the data is consolidated by the software and Form- 1 gets generated. A sample of the electronically generated Form- 1 is given below

<table>
<tr><td colspan="6">Sample copy of electronically generated application (Form-1)</td></tr>
<tr><td colspan="3">FORM 1
THE PATENTS ACT, 1970
(39 of 1970)
&
THE PATENTS RULES, 2003
APPLICATIONFORGRANTOFPATENT
[See sections 7,54 & 135 and rule 20(1)]</td><td colspan="3">(FOR OFFICE USE ONLY)
Application No.: ....
Filing Date: ....
Amount of Fee Paid: ....
CBR No.:...............
Signature:...............</td></tr>
<tr><td colspan="3"></td><td colspan="3"></td></tr>
<tr><td colspan="6">1. APPLICANT(S):</td></tr>
<tr><td>Sr.No.</td><td>Name</td><td colspan="2">Nationality</td><td colspan="2">Address</td></tr>
<tr><td></td><td></td><td colspan="2"></td><td colspan="2"></td></tr>
<tr><td colspan="6">2. INVENTOR(S):</td></tr>
<tr><td>Sr.No.</td><td>Name</td><td colspan="2">Nationality</td><td colspan="2">Address</td></tr>
<tr><td></td><td></td><td colspan="2"></td><td colspan="2"></td></tr>
<tr><td colspan="6">3. TITLE OF THE INVENTION:</td></tr>
<tr><td colspan="6">4. ADDRESS FOR CORRESPONDENCE OF APPLICANT / AUTHORIZED PATENT AGENT IN INDIA:</td></tr>
<tr><td colspan="6">5. PRIORITY PARTICULARS OF THE APPLICATION(S) FILED IN CONVENTION COUNTRY:</td></tr>
<tr><td>Sr. No.</td><td>Country</td><td>Application number</td><td>Filing Date</td><td>Name of the Applicant</td><td>Title of the Invention</td></tr>
<tr><td></td><td></td><td></td><td></td><td></td><td></td></tr>
<tr><td colspan="6">6. PARTICULARS FOR FILING PATENT COOPERATION TREATY (PCT) NATIONAL PHASE APPLICATION:</td></tr>
<tr><td></td><td></td><td colspan="2"></td><td colspan="2"></td></tr>
<tr><td colspan="3">International Application Number</td><td colspan="3">International Filing Date as Allotted by the Receiving Office</td></tr>
<tr><td colspan="3">PCT//</td><td colspan="3"></td></tr>
</table>

Contd...

7. PARTICULARS FOR FILING DIVISIONAL APPLICATION	
Original (first) Application Number	**Date of Filing of Original (first) Application**
8. PARTICULARS FOR FILING PATENT OF ADDITION	
Main Application / Patent Number	**Date of Filing of Main Application**

9. DECLARATIONS:

(i) Declaration by the inventor(s)

I/We ……………………………………………, is/are the true & first inventor(s) for this invention and declare that the applicant(s) herein is/are my/our assignee or legal representative.

(a) Date:-----

(b) Signature(s) of the inventor(s):...............

Name(s):

(ii) Declaration by the applicant(s) in the convention country

I/We, the applicant(s) in the convention country declare that the applicant(s) here in is/a my/our assignee or legal representative.

(a) Date: -----

(b) Signature(s): ....

(c) Name(s) of the signatory:

(iii) Declaration by the applicant(s)

I/We the applicant(s) hereby declare(s) that: -

- The complete specification relating to the invention is filed with this application
- I am/we are, in the possession of the above-mentioned invention
- The invention as disclosed in the specification uses the biological material from India and the necessary permission from competent authority shall be me/us, before the grant of patent to me/us.
- There is no lawful ground of objection to the grant of patent to me/us

Contd...

10. FOLLOWING ARE THE ATTACHMENTS WITH THE APPLICATION

Sr. No.	Document Description	File Name
1	Form 1	Form 1.pdf
2	Complete Specification	Complete specifications.pdf
3	Drawings	Drawings.pdf
4	Figure of Abstract	Abstract.pdf

I/We hereby declare that to the best of my/our knowledge, information and belief the fact and matters stated hering are correct and I/We request that a patent may be granted to me/us for the said invention.
Dated this (Final Payment Date): -------

Signature: ------------

Name:

To The Controller of Patents
The patent office at XXXX

This form is electronically generated

The above form is generated after consolidating the data entered directly in the software. So, while e-filing the applicant may not worry about the exact format as some of the commonly used forms are available directly in the software. In case of physical filing, the applicant has to type the desired information in prescribed format and take print of the same for communicating to the concerned patent office. The following points may be kept in mind while filling Form- 1 (either physically or through e-filing).

- Name of the inventor(s) and applicant(s) could differ. If the inventor themselves wants to possess the patent rights, then they may include their names as applicants also. It must be kept in mind that as explained in earlier chapter, applicant(s) is/are the actual owner of the patent rights. In case the inventors are employees and their research was funded by their organization then according to the existing IPR policy of their organization, the organization becomes the applicant and owns the patent right (if the patent gets granted in course of time). However, in such case the expenditure incurred for patenting is borne by the organization. Fees will vary based on the nature of the applicant (natural person, small entity or start-up).

- During e-filing, the names of applicant(s) and inventor(s) are separately added to the software in the prescribed format as presented by the software.
- In point number 04 (sample copy of electronically generated application), the address of the first inventor or address of the service of the organization (if organization is the applicant) must be mentioned. However, if the applicant has hired the services of an authorized patent agent, then the address of service of the said patent agent has to be mentioned, as all correspondence will now be made by the patent office to the hired patent agent since the applicants have duly transferred their power of authority to the patent agent for handling that particular patent application.
- Point 6-8 (sample copy of electronically generated application) may be left out unfilled by the applicant, if the applicant has nothing to declared regarding PCT international filing, divisional or patent of addition. For an ordinary Indian patent application for which no international filing has been done, these points can be ignored.
- By exercising Point 9(i) the inventors actually declare that they have carried out the invention by themselves and agreeing to transfer the rights to the applicants for applying for this patent and subsequently own the patent right in case patent gets granted in course of time. Transferring of right may not be necessary if the inventors and applicants are same. Point 9(ii) is required when the application is being filed in the convention country as per Paris Convention. If there is no such involvement, it may be ignored.
- Point 9(iii) consists of various declarations which the applicant wants to make. The applicant may choose from the list of declarations already available, the one that best suits with the nature of the application. If the invention is associated with the use of biological material (like plants) then declaration relevant to the above aspect must be made. The list of all declarations that are available are given below
    - I am/ We are in possession of the above-mentioned invention.
    - The provisional/complete specification relating to the invention is filed with this application.
    - The invention as disclosed in the specification uses the biological material from India and the necessary permission from the competent authority shall be submitted by me/us before the grant of patent.

- There is no lawful ground of objection(s) to the grant of the Patent to me/us.
- I am/we are the true & first inventor(s).
- I am/we are the assignee or legal representative of true & first inventor(s).
- The application or each of the applications, particulars of which are given in Paragraph-5, was the first application in convention country/countries in respect of my/our invention(s).
- I/We claim the priority from the above-mentioned application(s) filed in convention country/countries and state that no application for protection in respect of the invention had been made in a convention country before that date by me/us or by any person from which I/We derive the title.
- My/our application in India is based on international application under Patent Cooperation Treaty (PCT) as mentioned in Paragraph-6.
- The application is divided out of my /our application particulars of which is given in Paragraph-7 and pray that this application may be treated as deemed to have been filed on DD/MM/YYYY under section 16 of the Act.
- The said invention is an improvement in or modification of the invention particulars of which are given in Paragraph-8.

The applicant has to choose from the above-mentioned declarations, those which best matches with the invention filed for seeking patent protection.

- Point 10 (sample copy of electronically generated application) indicates in tabular form the list of files which have been uploaded by the applicant at the time of submission

8.1.2 Form-2

Complete specification (Form-2) is a mandatory form for ordinary patent application. Even for a provisional application, Form-2 is required but claims need not be mentioned. Form-2 is available in the submission software where the abstract, specifications and claims can be fed into the system in the allotted space. However, since specifications will contain complete experimental details with data in various forms, drawings or other details best required for carrying out the invention henceforth, such specifications and drawings to describe the invention must be uploaded separately. All kind of documents barring the affidavits and drawings shall be filed in Hindi or English unless permitted by the Controller to file in any other language. The typed text characters not less than 10 font size adjusted to one and half spacing and printed on one side of the paper only shall be used. Paper used should be of A4 size, white, non-shiny with a minimum margin of 4 cm from top and left and minimum 3 cm from bottom and right. The pages must be numbered in numerals aligned to center -bottom of every page. Line numbers must be provided to every fifth line of each page of the complete specification. Full names and complete addresses of applicants must always be mentioned. Any signature done other than in English or Hindi must be accompanied by a transcription of the name, either in Hindi or English, in block letters. The standard filing fee permits only 30 pages in the complete application form and inclusion of additional pages are subjected to extra payment. A sample Form-2 mentioning various headings under which the invention can be best described is given below for the understanding of the readers

Sample of Form 2

FORM 2 **THE PATENTS ACT, 1970** **(39 OF 1970)** **&** **THE PATENTS RULES, 2003** **COMPLETE SPECIFICATION /** **PROVISIONAL SPECIFICATION** *(Choose which ever is applicable)* **(See Section 10 and Rule 13)**
TITLE OF THE INVENTION **XXXXXXXXXXXXXXXXXXXXXXXXXXXXXX**
APPLICANTS **(name of applicants along with their address and nationality)**
The following specification particularly describes the invention and the manner in which it is to be performed Title of the Invention: **XXXXXXXXXXXXXXXXXXXXXXXXXXXXXX**
FIELD OF THE INVENTION: **BACKGROUND OF THE INVENTION** **OBJECTS OF THE INVENTION** **SUMMARY OF THE INVENTION** **BRIEF DESCRIPTION OF THE ACCOMPANYING DRAWINGS** **DETAILED DESCRIPTION OF THE INVENTION (include all available experimental details and data capable of best describing the invention)** **CLAIM(S)** **ABSTRACT** **ALL FIGURES/DRAWINGS (if any)**

Salient features of complete Specification (Form-2)

(a) Should completely describe all the operations involved in the invention, including the best method known to the applicant for performing and practicing the said invention.

(b) Must end with a single claim or multiple claims of the invention for which patent is being sought.

(c) Proper reference should be given regarding depositing any biological material (if involved in the filed invention) to any designated International Depository Authority (IDA). If there is a mention of a biological material (bacteria, fungi, eukaryotic cell lines such as plant spores, genetic vectors such as plasmids or bacteriophage vectors or viruses containing a gene or DNA fragments; organisms used for expression of a gene, plants) in the complete specification, and if the said material is not available to the public or its complete description is also not possible to provide in the specification as per the requirement mentioned in section 10(4)(a) and (b) of Indian Patents Act, such material should then be deposited with IDA under Budapest Treaty and as per Section 10(4)(ii) of the Indian Patents Act. As per 2016 data, there are 45 recognized IDA's in the world. **Microbial Type Culture Collection and Gene Bank (MTCC) at the Institute of Microbial Technology (IMTECH), Chandigarh and Microbial Culture Collection (MCC) in National Centre for Cell Science, Pune**, are the two designated IDA units in India. Applicants must deposit the respective biological material with a recognized IDA before filing of patent application and provide the reference of the same at the time of filing or within three months from date of filing indicating the details of the IDA and the date and accession number of such deposition. Also, the applicant must describe all the typical characteristics of the biological material in the complete specification so that it can be correctly identified. Access to the material deposited in the concerned IDA will be made available to the public after publication of the application. However, if the applicant files Form-9 (early publication), the said reference of deposition with IDA shall be given on or before the date of filing request for early publication. The geographical source/origin of any biological material mentioned in the specification must be disclosed in complete. If the specification involves usage of medicinal plants or microorganisms obtained from India, mandatory approval from National Biodiversity Authority (NBA), Chennai must be submitted any time before grant of patent, till then patent application may be declared as "found in order for grant" and final patent certificate will only be provided on submission of NBA approval. Such disclosure and deposition of sample with IDA brings completeness to a ordinary patent application enabling a person skilled in the art to reproduce and practice the invention by collecting the sample from IDA rather than starting from scratch or prepare the sample from nature.

(d) Abstract must be present.

(e) Avoid irrelevant information which may be misleading.

(f) In case of divisional application, reference of the basic application from which splitting is expected must be indicated. The same must also be practiced for the specification filed for patent of addition indicating the reference number of basic application.

(g) All pages must be signed, numbered and dated. However, if e-filing is done; the pages have to be signed by using digital signature.

Components of Form-2

1. **Title of Invention:** Title of the invention should not exceed beyond fifteen words. Title should be clearly indicating the subject matter of the invention and may disclose some exclusive features of the invention as well. Title should not make use of any imaginative expressions or present any ambiguity, rather should be precise and to the point. Details regarding the invention should be avoided in the title. The author may search from the Indian patent database (search method explained in a later chapter) some published and granted patents using specific keywords which has relevance to the said invention to get an idea about the nature of title used by various applicants.

2. **Field of the Invention:** This segment may begin with the statement "This particular instant invention relates to ……………………", indicating the subject matter of the invention; followed by benefits of the said invention which may likely mention the areas of application. The use of the invention must be clearly mentioned with sufficient indication about its industrial potential.

3. **Background of the Invention:** This segment explains the necessity of the said invention indicating what problems existed in the past and how this invention is likely to overcome them. Literature (prior art) relevant to the said invention must be discussed and explanation should indicate the major advancements or improvements achieved through the said invention. Distinct difference between the said invention and the available prior art should be visible from the explanation provided

4. **Objects of the Invention:** This segment can start with
   - "It is the principal object of the present invention to..........................."
   - "It is another object of the present invention to provide......................."
   - "It is a further object of the present invention to provide....................."

   The objectives which the invention has achieved can be listed out in the above-mentioned pattern indicating distinct advantages and advancements achieved from the already existing method (prior art) known to the public.
5. **Summary of Invention**: Applicant has to mention an executive summary of the invention which is being filed for grant of patent. Detailed experimental methodology and data need not be presented here, instead the major findings or revelation occurring from the said invention can be explained in light of the advantages exhibited by the invention. Different dynamics and applicability of the invention can be explained
6. **Brief Description of Drawings (if any)**: All the captions of drawings, figures and charts mentioned in the complete specification should be explained here
7. **Detailed Description of Invention**: Complete description of the invention must be given here in a manner such that any person skilled in the art upon reading the explanation should be able to perform the invention without any undue burden. All methodology adopted and findings of the experiments must be disclosed completely. Necessary explanation and observation from various drawing, flowcharts can be mentioned for easy explanation of the invention and any kind of reference of deposition of biological material with IDA and reference to basic application in case of divisional application, patent of addition (if any) must be mentioned here. If any sequence listing of nucleotides or amino acid sequence is to be disclosed, such disclosure must be submitted in computer readable text instead of giving in a printable form. A nucleotide sequence has to be mentioned with minimum 60 bases per line, with a space between each group of 10 bases. Any kind of computerized listing of sequence must be carried out by using committed software such as **Patent In**.
8. **Drawings**: All drawings should be mentioned in separate A4 size with distinct margin of minimum 4 cm from the top and left and 3 cm from bottom and right of the page. Dimensions should not be

mentioned on the diagram. The left top corner of the page bearing the drawing must contain the name of the applicant, the right top corner of the sheet must bear the total number of sheets used for exhibiting the drawings and the number of that respective sheet. The right bottom corner of the sheet must contain the signature of the applicant or his patent agent (if any). Description of the drawings should not be mentioned in the sheet containing the drawing.

9. **Abstract**: The word limit for abstract is 150 words. The abstract should start with the title of the invention and be drafted in such a way that it should reflect the summary of the complete specification. Clear indication of the technical field in which the invention has been made, the problems encountered with the earlier existing methods and the solutions provided through the current invention must be made. Chemical formula or equation may be mentioned if needed. The abstract should be instrumental in such a way that it should be identified in any search conducted in the technical field in which the invention has occurred.

10. **Claims [Section 10(4)(c)]**: They are the heart of the complete specification consisting of technical facts expressed wisely from a legal point of view and defines the boundary for patent protection. In future, such claims will define to what extent other competitors can invade the invention. Patent rights are not granted on the whole complete specification but rather on the claims that are mentioned at the end of the complete specification. Apart from the claims, the other details mentioned are used for evaluating the invention on the basis of novelty, inventive step, non-patentability aspects and industrial applicability. Claims should be drafted meticulously to cover all aspects of the invention. Claims which are well drafted, guard the invention from all possible angles from potential infringers. Until and unless the matter which is described in the complete specification is exclusively mentioned in the claims, the said aspect cannot be considered as protected under patent rights and is considered to be as good as being available in the public domain. Having said this, claims are like a protective wall around the main invention avoiding intrusions from infringers, it is also important to understand that too broad claims should not be made which probably claims more than what actually the invention is about. Such broad claims definitely block future improvement opportunities by other competitors which is not desirable for a healthy market scenario. Broad claims will be objected during the patent examination. On the other hand, too, narrow claims will not be effective enough to safeguard the invention from infringers.

Rather the applicant should focus on covering all features of the invention with multiple claims so that legal protection can be sought on all features of the invention. A patent claim(s) consists of three parts

- *The preamble*: It is an introductory line identifying the area of the invention and should be stated in consistent with the title of the invention. The purpose of the invention should be clearly reflected from the preamble. Also, it may state the object of the invention.

  Example: if the object of the invention is regarding making of tea, then the claim can begin with 'A method for making tea………". If the object of the invention is inventing a formulation for the treatment of jaundice, then the claim can be written as 'A composition for treating jaundice……"

- *Transitional phrase*: it is ascertained from the claims that the said invention involves only the said elements presented in the claims or may likely involve other similar undisclosed elements. The most common transitional phrase indicating a broader claim is 'comprising of' or 'consisting essentially' which indicates that the invention mainly comprises of the described elements but other elements could also be present. Transitional phrases indicating a narrow claim are 'consisting' which strictly indicates that the invention is only made of the prescribed elements as mentioned.

  Example: 'An apparatus/device comprising of ……..' is a broad claim (open ended) and shall also reflect involvement of those elements which are not mentioned in the specification. 'A composition for treating jaundice consisting of 60% component X, 30% component Y and 10% component Y' is a narrow claim (closed phrase) which is limited to the use of the said components only.

- *Body*: the sentence which follows the transitional phrase is the 'body' of the claim(s). The various features or elements of the inventions and their connectivity among them are generally mentioned in the body of the claim. Suppose if an invention reflects some major improvements over the existing prior art which is already available in the public domain, the body of the claim can be written as "An XXX process for <give the use of the process>, comprising …<mention the parts of the invention> + <also mention how these parts are connected to each other to complete the invention>".

Example: claim for invention of table can be drafted as 'an apparatus for holding objects, comprising: at least two legs and one configured top supported by at least two legs.

Types of Claims: Claims can be classified on the basis of Drafting, Inventions, Field and Structure.

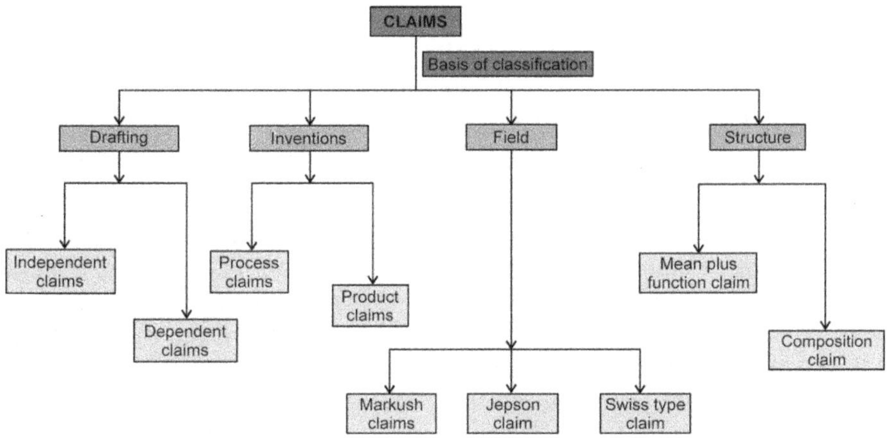

FIGURE 8.1 Types of Claims.

Independent claims: also known as 'Principal Claim' is the first claim and specifically dictate the primary and mandatory novel features of the most preferred embodiment(s) of the process, apparatus, device or product which has been filed for patenting. The said invention should be properly characterized with respect to the 'prior art', defining all the technical features necessary to describe the invention and establish the inventive step. Independent claims can be multiple in number and are generally broader in scope.

Example – a process for extraction of alkaloids from <name of the plant and its part> comprising .... <mention the features of the developed extraction process>.

Dependent claims: a dependent claim derives its existence from an independent claim. More specifically, the claims that follows after an independent claim is generally a dependent claim.

Example – the process as claimed in claim 1 (a method for extraction of alkaloid's from XYZ plant comprising of........) wherein the said invention...<mention the dependent features of the invention>

Product claims: directly mentions the actual product (said invention)

Example – a pharmaceutical composition comprising of ……..<mention the ingredients of the composition along with their percentage>

Process claims: directly claims a new process or method to achieve the desired output

Example – a process of preparation of a polyherbal mixture, said process comprises of the following steps ……<mention the parts of the invention leading to the desired output>. A method of making tea, wherein the said method comprises of: boiling the water; adding tea leaves; filtering the mixture, adding milk to the filtered mixture and adding sugar to the resultant mixture.

Markush claims: such type of claim is named based on the unique type of claims filed for US patent by an applicant called Eugene Markush in1920. Such claims indicate chemical structures along with their substituent groups. In such a claim, multiple parts of the claimed compound comprise of multiple functionally equivalent chemical entities. When a new organic compound is invented with no existence before, from such parent compound; derivatives may be made by possible substitutions of different functional groups. Markush claims allows claiming the basic parent structure along with the various substitutions like halogens, alcohols etc. supported by a single inventive process.

Example: an antiviral compound of the formula X-Y-Z wherein:

X is selected from C1-C5 alkyl group

Y is selected from C4-C8 carboxylic acid ester

Z is selected from substituted or unsubstituted phenyl group

Jepson claim: A Jepson claim style dictates in the preamble some kind of statement that relates to the state of the prior art (existing technology), and then claims an improvement over the existing prior art. The word "wherein..." is frequently used to frame the Jepson claim.

Example – in a process of making XYZ with elements 1,2,3 [available as prior art knowledge] wherein, the improvement comprises [the transitional phrase] of element 4 [the inventive element].

Swiss type Claim: is the style of presenting a claim for indicating new use of an already known substance. Such claims are not allowed as per the provisions mentioned in Section 3 of Indian Patents Act.

Means plus function claims: indicates that style of patent claim which does not specify a particular structure for an invention, but instead describes a means for achieving some function.

Example: if the object of the invention is related to the invention of an electric cooker, then claim can be written as 'A device for cooking rice, comprising a means for holding rice; and a configured installed heater for heating the rice-holding means'.

Composition claims: this style of presenting claim is used when the invention to be claimed has relevance to chemical nature of the materials or components used.

Example: A pharmaceutical composition used for the treatment of malaria comprising of component A and component B.

Such type of claim(s) is frequently subjected to objections during examination as such claims reflect only aggregation and cumulative effect of properties of the mixed ingredients which is not patentable under Section 3 of Indian Patents Act, until something more than a synergistic effect is exhibited.

Ideal characteristics of a claim(s);

- Claim(s) mentioned in complete specification must represent Unity of Invention (Section 10(5)) which means that it should relate to a single inventive concept
- Every claim is examined according to its own merit, rejection of one claim does not automatically reject other claims
- Claims should start with the word, 'I / We claim' as the case may be, depending on whether single applicant or multiple applicants have filed the patent application
- Should start from a fresh new page of the complete specification
- Should be serially numbered
- Each claim should be framed as a single sentence
- Initially only ten claims are allowed with standard filing fee. However, additional claims after this will be chargeable
- Claims must bear resemblance with specifications and should be supported with description mentioned in the specification
- Claims must not be speculative, rather specific

8.1.3 Form 3

As per the provisions mentioned in Section 8(1), applicant(s) if filing a patent application in respect of the same invention or substantially similar invention which has been filed or about to be filed in India, undertaking regarding the same in Form-3 must be submitted either along with the Indian application or within six months from the date of filing the application in India. In case the applicant(s) have not carried out any filing in foreign country, 'NIL' statement needs to be submitted in Form-3. The undertaking given in Form-3 basically contains detailed information of any foreign filing including the name of the foreign country where filed, application number and the status position of such application. It also contains a declaration by the applicant(s) that till a decision regarding his patent application is made, he will continue furnishing such information of foreign filing (if any) to the Controller. If the Controller himself asks for such information, the same has to be provided by the concerned applicant within three months from the receipt of such communication from the Controller.

<table>
<tr><td colspan="6">Sample of Form-3
FORM 3
THE PATENTS ACT, 1970
(39 of 1970)
and
THE PATENTS RULES, 2003
STATEMENT AND UNDERTAKING UNDER SECTION 8
[See Section 8; Rule 12]</td></tr>
<tr><td colspan="3">1. Name of the applicant(s)</td><td colspan="3">I / we, <full name of the applicant(s)>
All are Indian Citizens,
<address of all applicant(s)></td></tr>
<tr><td colspan="3">2. Declaration</td><td colspan="3">hereby declare:
that we who have made this application
No.....................................
Dated DD.**MM.YYYY**
lone/jointly
with.........................., made for
the
same/substantially same invention,
application(s)
for patent in the other countries, the
particulars of
which are given below:</td></tr>
<tr><td>Name of the country</td><td>Date of application</td><td>Application No.</td><td>Status of the application</td><td>Date of publication</td><td>Date of grant</td></tr>
</table>

Contd...

NIL	
3. Name and address of the assignee	That the rights in the application(s) have been assigned to **NONE** That we undertake that upto the date of grant of the patent by the Controller, we would keep him informed in writing the details regarding corresponding applications for patents filed outside India within six months from the date of filing of such application. Dated this Xth day of <Month>, YYYY
4. To be signed by the applicant or his authorized registered patent agent	
5. Name of the natural person who has signed	
	To The Controller of Patents, The Patent Office, at XXXX (depends on jurisdiction)

Point 2 in the above Form-3 indicates that no foreign filing has been carried out and henceforth 'NIL' has been recorded. But if foreign filing has been done, the necessary date must be entered as asked. If the applicant(s) have not carried out any foreign filing and is filing the patent application for their said invention for the first time in India, then Form-3 can be filed at the time of submission of patent application. However, later if the applicant carries out any foreign filing, he may furnish such information to the patent office of appropriate jurisdiction in Form-3. It may also be noted that additional time for filing Form-3 may be granted by the Controller if requested.

8.1.4 Form-5

Declaration of inventorship has to be filled in Form-5 as per the provisions mentioned in Section 10(6) of Indian Patents Act. This particular form is required also in case of filing in India by a foreign applicant as convention country or under PCT national phase filing by any foreign applicant. Controller may permit filing Form-5 within one month from the date of filing of complete specification, however, such request can be made to the controller by applying through Form-4. The best practice is to file Form-5 along with the complete specification.

Sample of Form-5

FORM 5

THE PATENTS ACT, 1970

(39 of 1970)

&

THE PATENT RULES, 2003

DECLARATION AS TO INVENTORSHIP

[See Section 10(6) and Rule 13(6)]

1. **I/We, <name of the applicant(s)>**hereby declare that the true and first inventor(s) of the invention disclosed in the complete specification filed in pursuance of our application numbered.........................dated DD.MM.YYYY is/are:

2. **INVENTOR(s)**

Name	Nationality	Address

Dated this Xth day of <Month>, YYYY.

To,

The Controller of Patents

The Patent Office,

XXXX (Delhi, Kolkata, Chennai, Mumbai depending upon the jurisdiction)

Signature

8.1.5 Form 28

This form is required only if the applicant belongs to the category of MSME (Micro, Small & Medium Enterprises)/Startup. Since the filing fee and subsequent other fees involved in the patent processing depends upon the category of the applicant (whether natural person or startup or organization) hence, Form-28 is required in case of startup's or MSME as a proof of their category of applicant in accordance with Rule 2(fa)/2 (fb). Form-28 can be filed at the time of submission of patent application or within one month from filing the complete specification.

<table>
<tr><td colspan="3">Sample copy Form-28
FORM 28
THE PATENTS ACT, 1970
(39 of 1970)
AND
THE PATENTS RULES, 2003
TO BE SUBMITTED BY A SMALL ENTITY / STARTUP
[See rules 2 (fa), 2(fb) and 7]</td></tr>
<tr><td>1</td><td>Insert name, address and nationality.</td><td>I/We
……………………………………………
……………………………………………
applicant/ patentee in respect of the patent application no. ………………. or patent no……………….. hereby declare that I/we am/are a small entity in accordance with rule 2(fa) or a startup in accordance with rule 2(fb) and submit the following document(s) as proof:</td></tr>
<tr><td>2</td><td colspan="2">Documents to be submitted</td></tr>
<tr><td></td><td colspan="2">i. For claiming the status of a small entity:</td></tr>
<tr><td></td><td colspan="2">A. For an Indian applicant: Evidence of registration under the Micro, Small and Medium Enterprises Act, 2006 (27 of 2006).</td></tr>
<tr><td></td><td colspan="2">B. In case of a foreign entity: Any other document.</td></tr>
<tr><td></td><td colspan="2">ii. For claiming the status of a startup</td></tr>
<tr><td></td><td colspan="2">A. For an Indian applicant: Any document as evidence of eligibility, as defined in rule 2(fb).</td></tr>
<tr><td></td><td colspan="2">B. In case of a foreign entity: Any other document.</td></tr>
<tr><td>3

4</td><td>To be signed by the applicant(s) / patentee (s) / authorised registered patent agent.

Name of the natural person who has signed.</td><td>The information provided herein is correct to the best of my/our knowledge and belief.

Dated this ……… day of …………. 20...
Signature ……………………</td></tr>
<tr><td></td><td>Designation and official seal, if any, of the person who has signed.</td><td>(Name)………………………
(Designation)…………………

To The Controller of Patents,
The Patent Office,
At………………………………";</td></tr>
</table>

8.1.6 Form 26

If the applicant(s) has hired the services of an authorized patent agent, the power of authority (power of attorney) shall be transferred to the patent agent vide Form-26 and has to be submitted within a period of three months from filing the complete specification. This form needs to be produced on a non-judicial stamp paper of minimum worth Rs 20. Thereafter, all sorts of communication by the patent office regarding the said application will be done with the authorized patent agent.

<table>
<tr><td colspan="2">Sample copy of Form-26
Rs. 20
INDIA NON JUDICIAL STAMP PAPER</td></tr>
<tr><td colspan="2">POWER OF AUTHORITY
THE PATENTS ACT, 1970</td></tr>
<tr><td colspan="2">I/We,
<name of the applicant>
&
<citizenship>
Hereby authorize <name of the patent agent>, all Indian nationals and all of <name of patent law firm with address> to act on my/our behalf as my/our patent agents for filing and prosecution of our application title "...................." and for obtaining letters, patent documents from Government of India in respect of the invention disclosed in the said application and for carrying out all necessary acts and to take all steps required therefor including appointment of substitute(s) wherever necessary, and confirm that all notices, requisitions and communications relating to our said application may be sent to such agent at the above address unless otherwise specified. We hereby revoke all previous authorizations, if any, in respect of the same matter of proceeding and assent to the actions already taken by them.
Dated this XthDay of MM, YYYY</td></tr>
<tr><td>Signature with full name off applicant</td><td>Signature with full name off applicant</td></tr>
<tr><td colspan="2">Notarization or legalization is not required</td></tr>
</table>

8.1.7 Form-18

The request for examination along with prescribed fee is filed through Form-18. Until the fee for examination has been deposited and request for examination through Form-18 have been made, examination cannot proceed post publication of the application. This is discussed in detail in the subsequent section of this chapter. Form-18 can be filed at the time of submission of application or even after the publication of the application. In-fact, Form-18 can be filed within 48 months from the date of filing, if not done so, the application will be deemed to be withdrawn by the applicant.

8.1.8 Priority Document

Priority documents are required for convention application filed in convention countries and for PCT National Phase Application. A priority document testifies the priority date which is the first filing date of the basic application filed in any convention or PCT signatory country. Subsequent filings in member countries within 12 months will enjoy the advantage of the priority date, for establishing the same a priority document is necessary which is to be submitted at the time of filing subsequent applications of the same invention in member countries. Priority documents are issued by the patent offices were filing of the basic application for the first time has taken place. Indian Patent Office has the facility of accepting digital priority document via the WIPO Digital Access Service (DAS) under the WIPO-INDIA Cooperation Agreement (initiated from 31st January 2018). Through this digital platform of DAS, the applicant(s) can request the patent office where the first filing of the basic application has taken place to add the priority document into the DAS system and provide the access code of the same to the applicant. The applicant then can hand over the access code to the Indian Patent Office (if any application is subsequently filed in India as convention application) for giving authorization to the Office to exchange the information through secure channels. Through this DAS system which is administered by WIPO, the applicant need not separately provide copies of priority document to all subsequent patent offices where convention or PCT National Phase Filing is being done. Rather, such priority documents can be exchanged between the convention patent office and the first filing office digitally through secure channels using an access code.

8.2 Enablement, Best Mode & Unity of Invention

According to the TRIPS agreement, Article 29(1), all member countries shall need to fulfill the enablement criteria before granting patent. Thus, enablement becomes a mandatory criterion, just like novelty an inventive step. Enablement indicates sufficiency of disclosure which means that the details of the invention should be disclosed to that extent, such that a person with ordinary skill in the art (area relevant to the field of the invention in which patent has been filed) can practice the invention or carry out the invention without any undue burden of experimentation.

Thus, when the patent expires, the complete specification should sufficiently dictate all aspects of the invention so that it can be practiced by others. Such enablement is key issue while dealing with biological material, as providing all details of the said microorganism on paper may not be possible. Henceforth, according to Budapest treaty, all member countries require to deposit their biological sample in the designated IDA and mention its reference in the complete specification while filing patent application.

Section 10(4) of Indian Patents Act describes Best Mode which makes disclosure of best mode of carrying out a particular invention as known to the inventor, mandatory during patent filing. However, European Patent Convention (EPC) does not obligate the applicant to disclose the best mode, enablement is sufficient according to their rule.

Failure to comply with the declaration of best mode in the complete specification could form one of the grounds for revocation of patent instituted by an interested person. But this provision is applicable only in India. In US, once the patent is granted, it cannot be challenged based on the reason that best mode was not declared. However, Section 64(1)h of the Indian Patents Act allows challenging the validity of a patent on the ground that the complete specification does not disclose the best mode as known to the applicant for executing an invention.

Example of best mode: if the applicant has developed some specific technicality for a device, which is very necessary to carry out the invention in the best possible way to obtain the best desired output, then it becomes obligatory to disclose such best mode. In case of process patent, if there involves a sample pre-treatment which can influence the net output of the process and if the inventor was aware of such a step, it becomes mandatory for the applicant to disclose such information in the complete specification during patent filing.

The examiner shall not carry out special investigation or test to detect the availability of the best mode, but rather shall assume that the best mode is disclosed in the application, unless evidence is presented by any interested person during opposition. It can be suggested that, the examiner will try to determine whether, at the time of application, the inventor knew of a mode of practicing the claimed invention which the inventor considered as the best possible mode. This is just a subjective enquiry since it makes an attempt to analyze the inventors state of mind at the time of filing the application. The examiner shall continue to assume that the best mode has been declared, unless the examiner has something to indicate that the inventor had in his possession the best mode, but did not disclose the same during filing. Such aspects (best mode and enablement) are used as tools by competitor's (most frequently by pharmaceutical companies) for invalidating the patent of others for retaining commercial benefit or for achieving complete market control for a particular product.

Unity of Invention [Section 10(5)] means that the claims mentioned in the complete specification evaluated either separately or mentioned in one single claim, should reflect to a single inventive concept. In case, the claims reflect multiple inventions in the same application, the Controller shall take a note of the same during FER and may ask the applicant to split the application and file them separately.

8.3 Application Submission

The patent application can be submitted both through physical filing and e-filing mode.

Physical filing: This is a traditional mode of filing; where documents in hard-copy as described in the above sections are prepared and then can be submitted either through post or in person at the counter of the appropriate patent office as per jurisdiction applicable. Separate fee and non-fee counters are present at the patent offices and accordingly the documents can be submitted as the case may be. It should be kept in mind that physical filing or paper-based filing will attract 10% additional fees on and above the standard filing fee. Jurisdiction or the patent office to which the application has to be submitted, depends upon the address documented in the application for the first applicant (described in earlier chapter). The documents can be submitted either through post or in person at the respective counter of the appropriate patent office. When documents are sent by post, the date of receipt of the documents by the patent office front desk is considered as the date of filing (priority date). Date of signing the documents or date of despatch through post by the applicant is not considered as filing date. However, patent agent should submit all documents only electronically after due authentication. Documents which are associated with submission of any kind of fee are received at the fee counter whereas, others at the non-fee counter. The office staff at the fee counter generates the Cash Book Receipt (CBR) and takes into record the CBR number, fee amount, patent application number, patent number (in case patent renewal fees) and other relevant information as the case may be. The hard copy documents so received either by post or in person are then sent to Electronic Data Processing (EDP) unit for digitization.

e-Filing: Web-based filing of patent application (e-filing) was started by Indian patent office in 2007 (https://ipindiaonline.gov.in/epatentfiling/goForLogin/doLogin). Applicants can register themselves as users and can own a personal cyber space in the patent office cyber environment.

The web-based filing provides a comprehensive software that guides the user through the process of filling all the entries as per Schedule 1 of the Patent Rules, 2003 along with providing necessary validations with patent office database with minimum transaction errors. The user first needs to register himself with the website using digital signature certificate (DSC). Subsequent multiple login post registration can be either through password mode or through DSC. Any applicant for the purpose of initial registration has to procure DSC of class III or II from authorized vendors mentioned in the patent office website. Actually, these vendors which are mentioned in the patent office website are also registered vendors with Ministry of Corporate Affairs. Names of such vendors are, (n)Code Solutions, TCS, Safe Scrypt and e mudhra. The cost of procuring a DSC under 'multipurpose' category for an individual for one year is approximately Rs. 3000 (including dongle and GST). User registration for application submission under the following user category can be done: Natural Person, Patent Agent, Organization/Legal entity, Small Entity and Startup. Barring patent agent everybody else have to initiate the registration initially by adding DSC. After successful configuration of DSC, user can enter the desired username (subjected to availability) & password and other factual data such as, name, address, email, mobile number for completing the registration process. Only patent agents can register themselves using their registration number issued by Indian patent office. Upon entering the number, the software validates the data and the name and address of the patent agent is displayed, the patent agent now can proceed for selecting the desired username and password thus completing the registration process. Once the registration is completed, the user can login using the password which was set during the registration process or may login through the digital signature mode. The following steps can now be performed post login

- A list of following options is displayed in the left side of the screen as shown below:

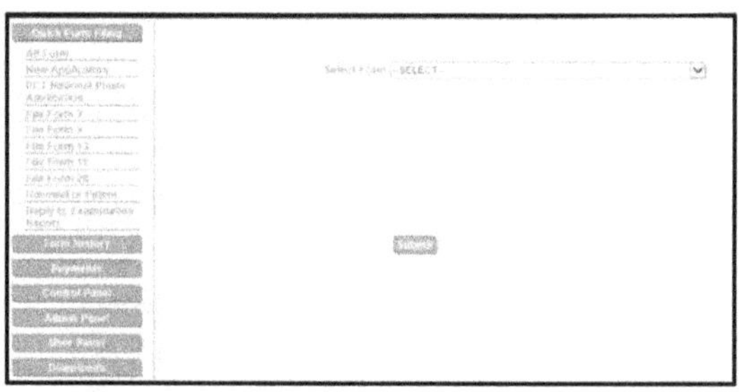

FIGURE 8.2 A real time view of the online submission of patent application. (e-filing) depicting various available options

- The user can now choose from the available options based on what exact task has to be performed. Either a new application filing can be started or pending forms for already submitted application can be uploaded or renewal fees of patent can be paid or suitable written reply to the examination report can be filed, likewise many such action related to patent handling can be performed through a click of a button.

- 'History Option' indicates all Forms which have been drafted and saved in the portal and discarded Forms as well
- 'Payments' option will provide the link to payment gateway so that necessary fees for different steps can be paid. All payment history is also stored in this section.
- 'Control Panel' contains links for changing the password or for renewing or updating the digital signature
- 'User Panel' contains the basic details of the user
- 'Download' contain essential items that are readily available for downloading like manual, and other utility items

The user has to fill up the desired Forms available in the module and save the file as draft copy (saved draft will be available in 'Form History'). After saving the draft, the user can upload the necessary documents by choosing the category of documents from the drop-down menu as shown below.

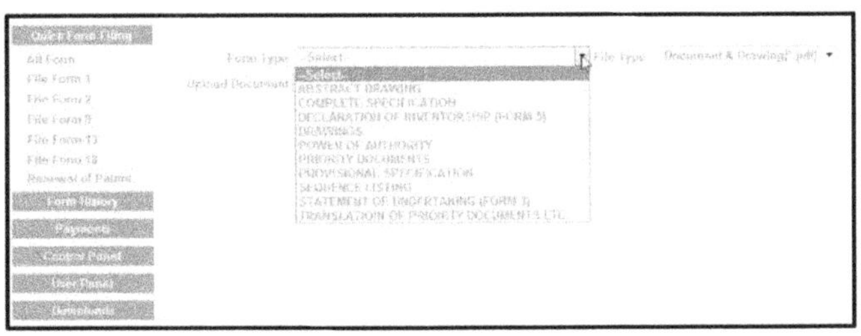

FIGURE 8.3 A real time view of the online submission of patent application (e-filing) depicting various documents which needs to be uploaded in the portal.

All the saved draft Forms will be available in a grid pattern in the 'Form History' option from which the author can chose the Forms and sign them using digital signature through 'sign document' option in the module. After digital signature is imposed on all documents, no alteration will be allowed by the system. The user now has to proceed to the 'payment' option in the module. The forms which are associated with payment needs to be 'checked-in' by the user and the fee is automatically calculated by the software. Payment can be done through credit card, debit card, internet banking and UPI, more than 70 banks are a part of the payment gateway. Payment is credited to Non tax receipt Portal – Bharatkosh gateway. Payment link is not available between 23:00 hrs –

00:30 hrs due to banking reconciliation process; however, the other modules of the submission portal will work and remain active round the clock barring notified maintenance period. If payment is successful; necessary message is displayed. Even though, the payment is successfully made, but the application number is generated after two days on successful reconciliation by the bank and realization of fee into Bharatkosh. A schematic flowchart of patent filing steps using e-filing mode (as explained above) is presented below for easy understanding of the readers.

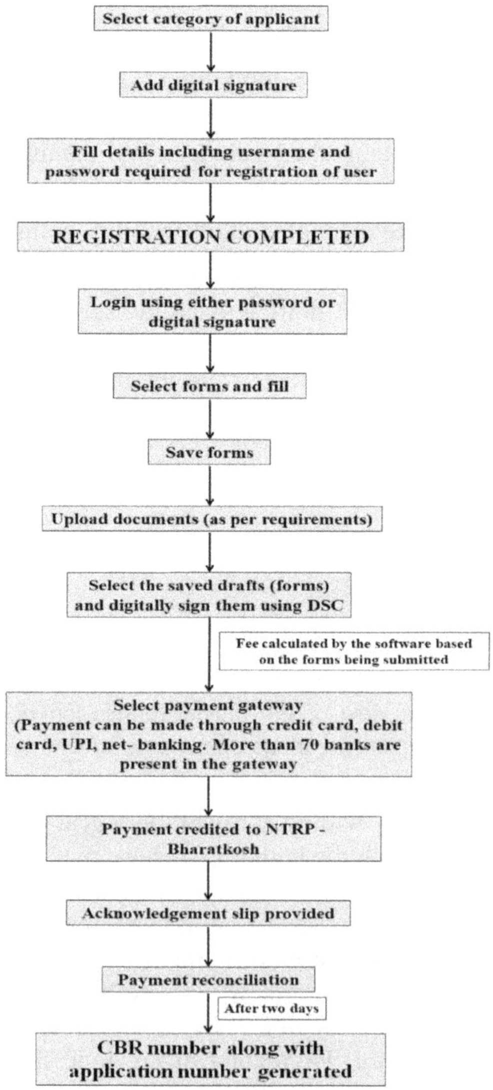

FIGURE 8.4 A schematic flowchart depicting online patent application submission process using e-filing mode.

8.4 Application Processing

In this stage preliminary screening and basic processing, regarding the application is undertaken. No detailed examination of the application is done at this stage. Scrutinizing the application becomes vital for paper filing as the applicant is likely to commit mistakes during physical filing. However, e-filing is very robust and software guided, hence scrutinizing becomes easy for such filing as most of the scrutiny and data consolidation is done through the software itself. Some basic scrutinization includes checks for,

- Numbering of the application, particularly those which are received as hard copy followed by subsequent digitization of the received documents
- International patent filing (if any)
- Ascertaining the technical field of the invention so that it can be allotted to a suitable examiner for the purpose of examination
- Any connection with defence purposes of the country and atomic energy
- Appropriateness of the abstract
- Whether the application has been submitted to the appropriate patent office as per the applicable jurisdiction, to be decided based on the recorded address of the first applicant.
- Signature available on all documents
- Proper filing of all Forms and fees.

The numbering of patent application is done as per the given format below,

YYYYJTNNNNNN

YYYY = Year of filing

J = jurisdiction, indicates to which patent office a particular application should be submitted (1 indicates Delhi, 2-Mumbai, 3-Kolkata & 4-Chennai)

T = indicates 'Type of application' (1-ordinary application, 2-ordinary-divisional application, 3-ordinary-patent of addition, 4-convention application, 5-conention-divisional application, 6-convention-patent of addition application, 7-PCT national phase application, 8-PCT national phase-divisional application, 9- PCT national phase application-patent of addition)

NNNNNN = this is a six digit running common serial number applicable to all the four patent offices

Example – Decoding the application number 202031000111. This particular application number indicates that the patent application was filed in the year 2020 at Kolkata patent office (henceforth, the recorded address of the first applicant belongs to a state which is covered under Kolkata jurisdiction), this is an ordinary patent application filed with complete specification having a running serial number of 111.

Secrecy Directions (Section 35) and Relevance with Atomic Energy (Section 4): Whenever a patent application is submitted either through paper filing or e-filing, a special team of the patent office carries out scrutiny and separates all those applications which are found to have relevance with India's defence purposes and atomic energy. If from the results of the initial scrutiny of the application, it becomes apparent to the Controller that the application has relevance with the defence purposes of the country, as notified by the Central Government, Controller will issue *secrecy directions* as per the provisions mentioned in Section 35 of Indian Patents Act, which will result in the prohibition of publication of the application after the standard course of 18 months' time period. This protocol is necessary as every citizen of sovereign nation must protect the security of their own nation. Upon imposing secrecy directions, the Controller shall refer the matter to the concerned office of the Central Government for scrutiny of the application. As long as the secrecy directions stays imposed, the publication of the application will not take place but the examination of the application as per Indian Patents Act may proceed, but Controller cannot take a final decision regarding the acceptance or rejection of the application unless he receives clearance regarding the secrecy directions imposed, from the Central Government. Central Government shall periodically review (at interval of six months) such provisions which may no longer serve to be prejudicial (harmfull) to the defence purposes of the country and may also take up any request for reconsideration of secrecy directions made by the applicant and forwarded by the Controller. Upon considering the merits of the secrecy directions, if the Central Government is satisfied that the filed invention is not prejudice to India's defence purposes, may provide instructions to the Controller who may then revoke the secrecy directions and inform the applicant accordingly. Once revoked, the final decision regarding the grant or rejection of the patent application can be taken after due examination as per patent norms. Indian resident cannot ordinarily undertake foreign filing without the permission of the Controller from Indian patent office as mentioned in Section 39 of Indian Patents Act. The best way to file a foreign application is to file a national application first and then wait for a minimum period of six weeks, if no secrecy directions are issued within this time period, then the applicant can proceed for foreign filing. Alternatively, the applicant may separately seek foreign filing permission from the Controller of the Indian patent office, such permission will only be granted post scrutiny of any secrecy issues (if any). Such permission is known as Foreign Filing License (FFL). Nevertheless, fast track procedures are available for obtaining FFL; if no secrecy directions are imposed. However, if secrecy gets imposed, the applicant may request to the Controller for reconsidering the decision, which the Controller shall forward to the Central Government or may wait for getting the application reviewed by the Central Government which is being done periodically or Government at every six months interval may consider revising those class of inventions which may no longer be prejudicial for the defence of the country. In such reviewing process, if the said invention is removed from the list of the inventions maintained by Central Government as prejudicial for India's defence purpose, secrecy shall then be revoked by the Controller after being instructed by the Central Government. Thus, through the provision of Section 39, no Indian resident can undertake foreign patent filing unless, filed first in India or without obtaining FFL. In such circumstances, no invention which has relevance with India's defence purposes can go outside India without proper monitoring by the Indian patent office. If during the continuation of the secrecy directions, the invention is used by or on behalf of the Government, the provisions of sections 100, 101 and 103 shall apply in relation to the use, considering the patent as if granted. Such above mentioned sections authorize the government or its authorized person to take charge of the invention and use it for its purpose, where such act will not constitute an infringement and the actual patentee in such cases is liable for compensation. If the Government takes charge of the invention and uses it for its own purpose and also because of the hardship faced by the applicant due to delay arising from the continuance of the secrecy directions, the Central Government may provide suitable compensation in way of solatium depending on the novelty and utility of the patent. If finally, the secrecy directions are revoked and the patent gets granted in due course of time, renewal fees for the time period for which secrecy directions were imposed will be waived. If the Central Government rejects the application under section 35 because of its involvement with the country's defence purpose, no appeal regarding the same will be entertained in any court of law or before the Appellate Board.

Atomic Energy: Post scrutiny, if the application is found to have relevance with atomic energy falling within the scope of Atomic Energy Act, 1962, the Controller shall forward the application to the Central Government (Department of Atomic Energy). The concerned department will ascertain the merit of the case and if the application is found to have relevance with atomic energy, necessary directions will be served to the

Controller. If the decision is negative, the Controller will then reject the application according to the provision mentioned in Section 4 of Indian Patents Act. The decision is not open to any contest or appeal.

Upon completion of the scrutiny, the document is stored in the form of an e-wrapper digitally in the server of the patent office for 18 months with no access to the public. Even though, the applicant has the application number, but no trace of the application can be found on the internet using that number as all applications are stored confidentially in highly secured servers of the patent office. However, the applicant can make use of this 18 months' time to take a decision to withdraw the application, if he desires so. Nevertheless, the option for withdrawing the application is open to the applicant till the grant of the patent. Request for withdrawal can be filed under section 11B(4) by applying in Form 29. If the application is withdrawn within the first fifteen months (within the 18 months lock period in the server) from the date of filing (assuming filing date is the priority date), the application will not be published. Moreover, if the request for withdrawal is filed before the generation of the first examination report, 90% of the examination fee is refunded. It should be strictly kept in mind by the applicant that necessary information to intimate the Controller regarding foreign filing of the same invention or substantially similar invention(s) must be conveyed to the Controller from time to time as per the provision of Section 8 of Indian Patents Act till the grant of patent. Non-compliance to this provision or any misrepresentation of fact under Section 8 may form a ground for revocation of patent at a later stage, if any such revocation request is filed by any opponent after the grant of patent.

8.5 Publication of Patent Application (Section 11A, Rule 24)

After the end of 18 months period, the application is now published at the earliest as per the provisions mentioned in Section 11A of Indian Patents Act. Barring secrecy directions, publication is a perquisite in-order to start the examination process. The publication of the application shall not take place under the following circumstances:

- When secrecy directions under Section 35 are imposed
- Application is abandoned because complete specification was not filed within twelve months from filing the provisional application
- Where complete specification was filed, but application withdrawn within first fifteen months of filing
- Application is rejected under Section 4 (relevance to atomic energy).

The publication takes place in the official journal of the Indian patent office which is published on weekly basis on every Friday. In case the applicant wants a faster processing of the patent application, can file Form-9 along with additional fee, under such circumstances the application will be published after one month and then can be queued up for examination, if request for such examination is made by the applicant. This accelerated system of publication is known as early publication (explained in earlier chapter).

Sample copy of Form-9

FORM 9

THE PATENTS ACT, 1970

(39 of 1970)

&

THE PATENTS RULES, 2003

REQUEST FOR PUBLICATION

[See SECTION 11A(2); Rule 24A]

1. Name, address and nationality of the applicant(s) 2. To be signed by the applicant or his authorized registered patent agent	I/we .... hereby request for early publication of my/our application for Patent No. ....dated ....under section 11A(2) of the act.
Dated this .... day of 20	
3. Name of the natural person who has signed	Signature ....
To The Controller of patents The Patent Office At .... (Delhi, Kolkata, Mumbai, Chennai)	

It should be kept in mind that such facility is only available with ordinary application where complete specification has been filed. If an applicant during submission has not filed Form-9, but wishes to get his application published at the earliest before 18 months, can do so by filing Form-9, any time before the publication and paying the additional fees. A glimpse of the official journal of Indian patent office and the pattern of publication with the type of contents published is shown below

Sample of cover page of the journal

OFFICIAL JOURNAL OF THE PATENT OFFICE

ISSUE NO. XX/YYYY FRIDAY DATE: DD/MM/YYYY

PUBLICATION OF THE PATENT OFFICE

The Patent Office Journal No. XX/YYYY Dated DD/MM/YYYY

Sample content of early publication of any application

Early Publication:

The following patent applications have been published under section 11A (2) of The Patents (Amendment) Act 2005 and rule 24A of The Patents (Amendment) Rules, 2006. Any person may file representation by way of opposition to the Controller of Patents at the appropriate office against the grant of the patent in the prescribed manner under section 25(1) of the Patents (Amendment) Act 2005 read with the rule 55 of The Patents (Amendment) Rules, 2006:

PATENT APPLICATION PUBLICATION Application No.YYYYJTNNNNNN A

INDIA

Date of filing of Application: DD/MM/YYYY Publication Date:DD/MM/YYYY

Title of the invention:

xxxxxxxxxxxxxxxxxxxxxxxxxxxxxxxxxxxxxxxxxxxxxxxxxxxxxxxxxxx

INTERNATIONAL CLASSIFICATION:	**NAME OF APPLICANT: XXXXXXX**
PRIORITY DATE:	

NAME OF PRIORITY COUNTRY:	
INTERNATIONAL APPLICATION NO:	*Contd...*
FILING DATE:	**Name of the**
INTERNATIONAL PUBLICATION NO:	**Inventor:**
PATENT OF ADDITION TO APPLICATION:	
NUMBER:	**xxxxxxxxxxx**
FILING DATE:	**xxxxxxxxxxx**
DIVISIONAL TO APPLICATION NUMBER:	
FILING DATE:	

Abstract:xxxxxxxxxxxxxxxxxxxxxxxxxxxxxxxxxxxxxxxxxxxxxxxxxxxxxxxxx xxxxxxxxxxxxxxxxxx

No. of Pages : 18 No. of Claims : 14 (representation only)

The Patent Office Journal No. 08/2021 Dated 19/02/2021

The Patent Office Journal No. 08/2021 Dated 19/02/2021

Sample content of normal publication (after 18 months) of any application

PATENT APPLICATION PUBLICATION	Application No.YYYYJTNNNNNN A
INDIA	
Date of filing of Application: DD/MM/YYYY	Publication Date: DD/MM/YYYY
Title of the invention:	
INTERNATIONAL CLASSIFICATION:	**NAME OF APPLICANT:XXXXXXXXXX**
PRIORITY DATE:	

Contd...

NAME OF PRIORITY COUNTRY: .... INTERNATIONAL APPLICATION NO: .... FILING DATE: .... INTERNATIONAL PUBLICATION NO: .... PATENT OF ADDITION TO APPLICATION: .... NUMBER: .... FILING DATE: .... DIVISIONAL TO APPLICATION NUMBER: .... FILING DATE:	**Name of the Inventor:** xxxxxxxxxxxxxx xxxxxxxxxxxxxx

Abstract:

xxxxxxxxxxxxxxxxxxxxxxxxxxxxxxxxxxxxxxxxxxxxxxxxxxxxxxxxxxxxxxxxxxxxxxxxxx xx

No. of Pages: 18No. of Claims: 14 (representation only)

The Patent Office Journal No. 08/2021 Dated 19/02/2021

The Patent Office Journal No. 08/2021 Dated 19/02/2021

The official journal publishes patent information related to publications (early and normal) from all patent offices of India, applications for restored patents which had lapsed and publication regarding intimation of grant of patent from all patent offices are also published. The various types of contents which are published in the official journal of the patent office are presented below in a tabular form

TABLE 8.1 Various types of contents which are published in the official journal of Indian patent office.

S. No.	Type of content published in the official journal of patent office
1	Early publication for applications filed at Delhi, Mumbai, Chennai & Kolkata patent office separately
2	Publication after 18 months for applications filed at Delhi, Mumbai, Chennai & Kolkata patent office separately
3	First examination reports issued for applications filed at Delhi, Mumbai, Chennai & Kolkata patent office separately

Table 8.1 ***Contd...***

S. No.	Type of content published in the official journal of patent office
4	Publication regarding restoration of lapsed patents (initially the concerned application filed by the applicant for restoration of lapsed patent is published followed by the intimation of restoration if allowed by the Controller)
5	Amendments made to a granted patent under Section 57 and 59
6	Amendments made to a granted patent under Section 78 where any clerical error correction have been allowed by the Controller
7	Publication indicating grant of patent for applications filed at Delhi, Mumbai, Chennai & Kolkata patent office separately. Patent number, application number, date of application, priority date, title of invention, name of applicant(s) along with jurisdiction where filed, is published in a tabular form
8	Applications made for grant of compulsory license
9	Details of application for which request for examination was not filed within 48 months of priority date
10	Applications for which first examination report was generated but reply not filed within the prescribe time limit
11	Publication of designs
12	Publication of copyright
13	Proceedings being cancelled under the Designs Act, 2000
14	Registration of designs

Implications of publication of patent application:

- All documents filed with the application are now available to the public and can be downloaded free of cost from the website. Copies of the documents can be obtained from the patent office on payment basis.
- Application becomes eligible for examination. However, examination will commence only when the request for examination is filed in Form-18 and examination fee is paid.
- The depository institution where the biological material (if any involved in the invention and mentioned in the complete specification) has been deposited, will now be available to the public.
- The application shall have the same privilege as applicable for granted patent. At this stage if any competitor invades the invention, it shall constitute an infringement considered from the date of publication of application. The applicant can make the invention commercially available with 'patent pending' remark on the product.
- There is a minimum time gap of six months from the date of publication and grant of patent.

- Pre-grant opposition begins and will continue till the grant of the patent. Any person on seeing the details of the invention posted on the patent office website can file a pre-grant opposition.

8.6 Examination & Grant

Examination of a patent application will take place only when it is published and request for examination has been filed in Form-18 along with prescribed fees anytime within 48 months from the date of filing (assuming the same to be priority date). In case secrecy directions are imposed, request for examination may be made within six months from the revocation of such directions or within 48 months from the date of filing whichever is later. A sample representation of Form-18 is given below.

<table>
<tr><td>
Sample of Form-18

FORM 18

THE PATENT ACT, 1970
(39 of 1970)
&
THE PATENTS RULES, 2003

REQUEST/EXPRESS REQUEST FOR EXAMINATION OF APPLICATION FOR PATENT
[See section 11B and rules 20(4) (ii),24B (1) (i)]
</td></tr>
<tr><td>
1. APPLICANT(S)/OTHER INTERESTED PERSON(S):
(a) Name: ....
(b) Nationality: ....
(c) Address: ....

(d) Date of Publication Under Section 11A:
</td></tr>
<tr><td>
2. STATEMENT IN CASE OF REQUEST FOR EXAMINATION MADE BY THE APPLICANT(S)
I/We .... hereby request that our application for patent invention number ....filed on DDMMYYYY for the titled .... shall be examined under section 12 and 13 of the Act.
</td></tr>
</table>

Contd...

3. **ADDRESS FOR SERVICE: <address of patent agent if any>**
Dated this (Final Payment Date):------------ Signature Name of the Signatory
To, The Controller of Patents, The Patent Office At XXXXX (name of the patent office where filed)
This form is electronically generated

If no request for examination is filed within the prescribed time limit, the application is considered to be withdrawn. There is a scheme of expedited examination where examination will be conducted with priority in express mode. For such purpose Form- 18A along with fee has to be filed. However, Controller may limit the number of expedited requests for examination for a particular year. It is not necessary that request for examination will be filed by the applicant only, but any interested person even not related to the applicant can place the request along with fees. In such case the examination report is communicated to the applicant only and intimation of the same is just given to the interested person who has filed the request. The applications are queued up for examination in the order in which the request for examination has been made. The earlier the applicant files such request, the faster the application is taken up for examination. Noteworthy, to mention that the applicant need not wait for publication of the application, but can file the request for examination (Form-18 or 18A) at the time of submission also. A separate numbering of the application is undertaken (without changing the basic patent application number) for queuing up the application for the purpose of examination. The numbering pattern is explained as below,

Pattern: **RYYYYJNNNNNN** **R** = indicates request for examination, if 'R' is replaced by 'E', it indicates expedited examination request **YYYY** = year of filing **J** = indicates jurisdiction for patent application (patent office where the application was filed for the first time) **NNNNNN** = indicates six digit running serial number for all patent offices

The filed patent application is then refereed to the examiner by the Controller for conducting both formal and substantive examination within one month from the date of publication or making such request in Form-18, whichever is later. The allotment to examiner depends on the field of invention and specialization of the examiner. There are some core groups of examiners belonging to a particular specialization namely, Chemistry and allied subjects, Biotechnology, microbiology and allied subjects, Electrical, Electronics & related subjects and Mechanical and other subjects. These are broad groups and any invention as deemed fit by the Controller may suitably be allotted to any examiner from a particular specialization to which the invention has relevance. Apart from these specializations which depend on some formal course curriculum which might have been studied by the examiner during graduation, post-graduation or PhD level, special examination team for evaluating applications related to traditional knowledge may also be constituted, as traditional knowledge is not a part of any routine curriculum which could have been studied by the examiner during their formal education. The application is assigned to a specific module of the examiner who can access the details of the application through the office server on his computer. The examiner submits his report to the controller based on the patentability issues and other matters like pre-grant opposition of the invention within one to three months from the date of assignment of such application by the Controller. Upon receiving the report from the examiner, the Controller within one month from the date of disposal of the report (time taken by the controller to study the report issued by the examiner, which is generally one month) shall communicate such report to the applicant or his patent agent.

Pattern of examination: The examination of the patent application is undertaken as per the provisions mentioned in Section 12 of Indian Patents Act. The examiner conducts a thorough search on matters related to the invention as per the provisions mentioned in section 13 of Indian Patents Act. The patent examiner primarily looks into the following aspects during examination of the application,

- If there is any lawful ground of objection to the grant of patent
- Has been anticipated by publication before the filing date of the application
- Such invention if claimed in any complete specification filed for patent anywhere in the world or mentioned in any claims filed in any complete specification submitted in India before the filing date of the concerned application
- Determination of inventive step
- Non-patentability aspect as mentioned in Section 3 of Indian Patents Act.

The format of examination of the patent application can be classified into two categories namely, Formal classification and Substantive classification.

Formal classification: the following checks are conducted,

- Eligibility of the applicant to apply for patent.
- Appropriateness of all forms and documents submitted.
- To decide on matters related to jurisdiction which is to ascertain if the application has been filed at the appropriate patent office in accordance with the address documented for the first applicant. For foreign applicant who do not have any place of business or domicile in India, address of service in India as declared by the applicant has to be taken into consideration for deciding at which patent office the application must be filed.
- To determine if the complete specification has been filed within 12 months of filing provisional application (if any) so that priority date advantage can be granted to the applicant.
- If the application is being handled by a patent agent, it is necessary to validate the registration of the patent agent and also to check if Form-26 (power of Authority) in original have been filed.
- To determine if Proof of Right to make an application has been duly signed (mentioned in Form-1).
- To check the availability of Form-3, Form-5 and Form-18.
- Check for correctness of fees paid.

Substantive examination: The examiner tries to understand the completeness of the disclosure. The invention should be disclosed in such complete manner including the best mode of its operation, so that a person with average skills in the art can carry out the invention without undue burden of experimentation. Deposition of any biological material (if any) at appropriate IDA must be done and proper reference of the same should also be mentioned with description of its geographical source as well. The description of the invention should be simple and well established scientific and technical terms should only be used. Use of complicated technical term may be avoided as far as possible. Claims are meticulously examined because they actually define the boundary of the patent right. Examiners determines the broadness, clarity and preciseness of the claims and its appropriateness in relation to the invention so that no unrelated matter are included in the claims filed. Too broad claims going beyond the boundaries of the invention shall be objected during the examination. Unity of the invention is also taken into account. The application filed should reflect a single inventive concept. Multiple inventive concepts in a single application will be objected by the examiner and splitting of the application may be asked by the examiner during preparing his report.

Examination of patentability criteria, novelty, inventive step and industrial applicability: The explanation provided under chapter

'Patentable Subject Matter' may be considered by the readers for understanding the examination pattern. Most of the objections raised by the examiners pertains to this section. The prior art search results obtained by the examiner forms the basis of such objection. The patent examiner determines the level of closeness of the said invention to that of the information available from prior art and makes an attempt to understand that from the information available from prior art, will it be possible for a person with average skills to practice the invention. Such judicious thinking leads to determination of inventive step. Examiner will also try to find out, if the said invention is already in use in any part of the world. The examiner will also try to check, if the said invention has any relevance to the category of non-patentable inventions mention under Section 3 of Indian Patents Act.

After the completion of the examination, the First examination Report (FER) containing all the objections raised by the examiner on matters as mentioned above is generated, which is communicated to the applicant for filing response. FER may also contain instructions for making amendment in the claims and other parts as specified by the examiner. All such communications take place through email and also the matter is uploaded on the applicant's page on the website. The applicant has to provide a written clarification to the objections raised in FER within six months (extendable by three months through filing Form-4) from the date of issuance of FER, failing which, the application shall be considered to have been abandoned. Upon receiving the reply from the applicant within the given time frame, the application along with the reply is studied, if satisfied with the clarification and amendments which were instructed (if any), the Controller grants the patent. However, if not satisfied with clarifications or if the applicants contest any of the objections raised in FER, a hearing through video-conferencing shall be offered on payment basis. After completion of the hearing, written statement of the arguments presented by the applicant has to be filed within fifteen days from the date of hearing. If satisfied with the written submission and amendments (if any), the Controller may grant the patent or else the application is rejected. Patent is not refused without giving sufficient opportunity to the applicant to present a defence and such refusals are open to appeal before Intellectual Property Appellate Board (barring refusal on ground of having relevance to India's defence purposes and atomic energy). Once the final decision is reached for grant of patent, and if any external obligation is pending from applicant's side like submission of NBA approval, the issued order could be "found in order for grant". Upon completion of the pending obligations from the applicants end, the patent is finally granted and patent certificate is digitally generated.

A patent is finally granted after occurrence of the proceedings mentioned above and when the filed patent application is not refused by the Controller and not found to contravene any of the provisions and rules mentioned in the Indian Patents Act. Date of grant is actually the date on which the patent actually has been granted by the Controller, but the protection starts from the date on which the patent application was filed or the priority date whichever is earlier. Henceforth, an applicant after applying for patent need not wait till the grant of the patent but can commercialize the product with an indicator 'patent pending', as in due course of time when the patent gets granted, the protection will begin from the date on which the filing took place and after filling the applicant shall enjoy the privilege what he should have enjoyed if the patent would have been granted. Henceforth, any delay in obtaining the patent will not actually affect the applicant in any means. Potential invasion of the invention shall constitute an infringement from the day the publication has taken place but such infringement proceedings can only be initiated after the grant of patent. Similar to patent publication, intimation regarding granted patents is also published in the official journal of the patent office. Every patent, post grant is allotted a serial number and subsequently entered in the e-register on the day of grant itself. The e-register of patent, shall contain the name, address, nationality of the patentee, title of the invention, dates of grant and filing, status of renewal and fees paid for the purpose of renewal and details of the proceedings continuing before the Controller related to the said patent. Extracts obtained from the e-register is admissible before the court of law. The complete specification and patent certificate is available in the public domain through patent website. No delivery of patent certificate is made to the applicant or to his patent agent (if any). All patent certificates are generated electronically and uploaded on the patent website. As soon as the patent is granted, it is recorded in the patent e-register and as a result from the same date, the patentee has to pay the accumulated fee for renewal of patent within three months from the date of entry in patent e-register which is further extendable by six months on request by the applicant. Even though, patent has been granted for an invention (process, product, apparatus, machine or any other article), it still can be used without permission from applicant and not causing an infringement, if used by the Government for its own purpose and by any person for the purpose of experiment or for imparting education and learning to the students (Section 47 of Indian Patents Act). However, barring the above clause, the patentee shall have exclusive rights as granted under Section 48 of Indian Patents Act on the patented invention and any attempt of unauthorized use of the said product or process and its commercialization in India shall constitute an infringement. If for a granted patent, multiple patentee (applicants) is involved, each of them irrespective of their order of names mentioned in the application shall hold equal rights on the patent, unless a separate declaration deed regarding distribution of patent rights have been executed by the applicants (Section 50). When there are joint owners for a patent, license to a third party cannot be granted without the consent of all the co-owners involved. At the event of the patent being sold after obtaining the consent of all the owners involved, the person purchasing the patent while dealing with one of the owners shall be entitled to deal in the same manner as he would have done if there were a single owner of the said patent. The general law of ownership applicable to any movable property shall also apply in case of patent. The term of granted patent is for 20 years from the priority date of the application subjected to payment of renewal fees on time. Patent rights are considered to be in force as long as renewal fees is paid in advance on regular basis. Patent renewal fees starts from the third year of the patent counted from the date of filing. There is a provision of consideration of six months delay in payment of renewal fess along with penalty, which increases with every month's delay. Patent is liable to lapse, on account of non-payment of renewal fees. Renewal fees are different for different category of applicant.

8.7 Post Grant Activities Open to Applicant

1. *Renewal*: As mentioned above, renewal fee becomes applicable from the third year of patent calculated from the date of filing. Patent granting is a lengthy procedure so it is likely that patent may be granted after two years from the date of filing. Under such circumstances whenever the patent gets granted, the accumulated renewal fee from the third year (calculated from the date of filing) needs to paid by the applicant within three months from the grant of patent as per provision mentioned in Section 53 of Indian Patents Act. In case of event of the patent being granted within two years (possible only when early publication takes place), renewal fees shall be only applicable from the third year to be paid in advance. Renewal fees for patent of addition is not required. Nevertheless, if the patent gets lapsed due to non-payment of renewal fees, the applicant can apply for restoration in Form-15 within eighteen months from the date of lapse as per the provisions mentioned in Section 60 of Indian Patents Act. However, such application should well be supported with justification citing the delay in payment of renewal fees with necessary evidence. The Controller shall allow the submission only when he feels that the delay was unintentional and the applicant upon overcoming the reason causing such delay has filed for restoration immediately. A publication for restoration of the application shall follow in the official journal of the Indian patent office. A sample of Form-15 is given below.

<table>
<tr><td colspan="2" align="center">FORM 15
THE PATENTS ACT, 1970
(39 OF 1970)
&
The Patents Rules, 2003
APPLICATION FOR THE RESTORATION OF PATENT
[See section 60; rule 84]</td></tr>
<tr><td>1. Insert the name, address, nationality of the applicant(s)</td><td>I/We...hereby apply for an order of the Controller for the restoration of patent No. .... Dated .... granted to ....

The circumstances which led to the failure to pay the renewal fee for the year .... on or before .... are as follows: ....

I/we declare that I/we have not assigned the patent to any other person(s) and that the facts and matters stated herein are true to the best of my/our knowledge information and belief.
Dated this......... day of ....20...</td></tr>
<tr><td>2. To be signed by the applicant(s) or his authorized registered patent agent</td><td>Signature ....</td></tr>
<tr><td>3. Name of the natural person who has signed</td><td>Name ....</td></tr>
<tr><td colspan="2" align="right">To
The Controller of patents
The patent Office ....</td></tr>
</table>

In case the Controller is not satisfied after studying the statement along with evidence given by the applicant for restoration, the Controller shall issue a notice reflecting the same to the applicant. If within one month of receiving the notice, the applicant can request for a hearing to present his arguments. Upon completion of the hearing, the Controller shall dispose of the application by rendering his final decision as per the provisions mentioned in section 61 of Indian Patents Act. In both the case of acceptance or rejection of restoration, the same shall be duly published in the official journal of the Indian patent office. Any interested person can contest the decision of restoration by applying in Form-14 within two months from the date of publication of the decision in the official patent journal. An interesting fact comes up here on what happens if some competitor starts using the invention during the period when it was deemed to be lapsed, due to non-payment of renewal fees. If such usage by others takes place in that particular passage of time (from the date of lapse to the date of publication of restoration statement in official journal of the patent office) and then the patent happens to be restored later, such activity shall not constitute an infringement and no legal suit can be initiated. However, along with the restoration orders of the Controller, specific provisions on protection of the persons who had begun using the invention during the period of lapse, shall be duly mentioned.

2. *Transfer of rights* (Section 68 & 69): After acquiring a patent, the patent rights can be either assigned, licensed or transmitted by operation of law to a third party who was not involved with the said invention at the time of filing of patent application. However, such act of transmitting patent rights shall be only valid when the conditions and all provisions involved are mentioned in writing through a deed and executed legally.

    - *Assignments*: patentee transfers wholly or partially patent rights to another person (assignee) who then becomes legally empowered to prevent others from exercising the said invention which is patented. Assignments can be of three types such as, Legal assignment, where the person to whom the patent rights are assigned (assignee) becomes the owner or co-owner of the patent and has the right to get his name entered in the register of patent in the capacity of owner by applying through Form-16. In case of Equitable assignments, a definite share of the patent rights is assigned to the assignee, but in such case the assignee cannot have his name entered in the register of patent as owner but the assignee may have notice of his interest in the patent recorded in the register. Mortgages are another type of assignments, where wholly or partially patent rights are transferred to the assignee in return of some payment made by the assignee. Once the payment is returned back to the assignee, the patent rights are restored upon the original patentee.
    - *Licenses*: License is a written agreement between the patentee and licensee based upon some mutually agreed terms (like sharing of royalty) whereby the patentee grants a license under Section 70 of Indian Patents Act. By virtue of this license, the licensee acquires authorization to practice the invention and earn

commercial benefits out of it. There are four types of license. Voluntary license is based on mutual agreement between patentee and licensee, whereby the licensee can commercially practice the invention based on agreed terms including sharing of royalty. Controller or Central Government has no role to play in this case. Statutory licenses are those where Central Government authorizes a third party to commercially make use of the invention. Consent of the patentee is not mandatory in this case. Compulsory licenses are a good example of statutory license. Any interested person can apply for such license after three years have been completed from the grant of a particular patent as per provision of Section 84 of Indian Patents Act, on grounds that such patented invention has still not been made available to the public, or the patented invention even though available, is priced exorbitantly. In case of pharmaceuticals, for manufacturing any drug in the health interest of the public, such licenses can be granted to a third party by the Central Government. In exclusive licensing, all the rights are transferred to a third party except the title. It means that the licensee can commercially exploit the invention but cannot further license it to another person. Such right is exclusively given to the licensee and cannot be further transmitted.

- *Transmission by operation of law*: This occurs when the patentee dies, and the rights are transferred to his legal representative. During bankruptcy of a company having patent, the rights are accordingly transferred by the action of law.

The basic advantage of licensing is that, it becomes very difficult for the patentee to extract full commercial benefit out of the invention. Many manufacturing risks are involved and manufacturing at a large scale also may not be possible by the patentee due to lack of fund. In such cases, licensing is the best option where temporary right to commercially exploit the invention can be given to a third party in exchange of a healthy royalty. However, during the license period, the patentee has no control either partially or fully over his own invention. The major difference between licensing and patent assignment is that, in case of licensing temporary transfer of rights takes place for commercial exploitation in exchange of royalty (patentee in this case is still the owner of the patent). However, in case of assignment, permanent transfer of ownership (complete or partial) may take place on exchange of onetime payment.

3. *Surrendering of patent*: The patentee, may at any time, if wishes to surrender his patent, he may apply in writing (no particular Form is specified) to the Controller. Controller upon receiving such request, may publish the same in the official journal of the patent office and

also inform all persons who appears in the register having interest in the patent. If no contest is made by any interested person, the Controller shall revoke the patent and publish such revocation order in the official journal.

4. *Intimation regarding working of patent*: The controller may ask for information regarding the commercialization of the patent according to Section 83 of Indian Patents Act. The patentee or the licensee shall provide such information if asked for, within two months from the date of such notification. In general, the patentee shall provide information regarding the extent to which commercialization of the patent has been carried out in Form-27, in respect to every calendar year and within three months from the end of one particular calendar year.

5. *Amendments*: Changes in the complete specification or in any documents to the extent of being a disclaimer or correction may be allowed at the discretion of the Controller as per the provision mentioned in Section 57 & 59 of Indian Patents Act. Such amendments in complete specification, which would make the amended specification to claim something new which was not previously included in the complete specification, shall not be allowed. Amendments may be published in the official journal which is also open to contest (opposition can be filed in Form-14). Allowed amendments shall be published in the official journal. However, if any legal proceedings (infringement suit, revocation proceedings) are pending related to the patent, amendments shall be refused by the Controller.

6. *Alteration in register of Patents*. All information from cradle to grave related to a granted patent is stored in the e-register including matters related to ongoing proceedings of the patent before the Controller. If the patentee desires to change name, nationality, address (including address of service) already entered in the register of patents, may do so by applying to the Controller with necessary evidence supporting the changes. The Controller, if satisfied under the provisions mentioned in Section 67 of the Indian Patents Act, may allow such changes. Necessary fee may have to be paid by the patentee. Such entries in the e-register are available for public inspection through the official website of the Indian patent office. However, for rectifying any entry in the e-register of patents, which the applicant feels has been wrongly entered or lacks sufficient disclosure, may apply to the Intellectual Property Appellate Board under Section 71 of Indian Patents Act. Such request is subjected to hearing before the Appellate Board in presence of the Controller.

Acquisition of patent by Central Government: Central Government in certain circumstances, if considers a particular patented invention to be useful for public purposes, may acquire such patent from the patentee under Section 102 of Indian Patents Act by publishing a notification to that effect in the Official Gazette. On acquisition, all the rights are then transferred to the Central Government. When such acquisition takes place, Central Government may pay suitable compensation to the patentee. However, such acquisition is open to appeal before High Court.

CHAPTER 9

Opposition and Revocation

Patent application during the ongoing process of examination for grant of patent and even after the patent has been granted, in both circumstances filing of suitable opposition is possible. The basic objective behind opposition is to prevent inventors from wrongfully or unlawfully obtaining a patent for an invention. There are two types of opposition namely, pre-grant and post-grant opposition which can be filed at different stages of patenting. Two types of results are possible from any opposition, either the opposition persist, resulting in rejection of the application (if patent not yet granted)/patent (if already granted) or opposition may be overruled resulting in continuation of the application or patent as the case may be. Opposition can be filed by any person/ interested person in prescribed form and upon payment of necessary fee.

9.1 Pre-Grant Opposition

Such type of opposition can be filed by any person after publication of patent application under Section 11A and before the grant of patent. Any person can file an opposition by filing Form-7A based on the grounds mentioned in Section 25(1) and has to provide a copy to the applicant as well. Grounds of filing a pre-grant opposition as mentioned in Section 25(1) are as follows,

- Patent was wrongfully obtained from some other person
- Any of the act which constitute an anticipation of the patent may have taken place before filing of the patent
- Invention is already in use in public domain
- Invention being obvious lacks inventive step
- Subject matter involved in not an invention within the true meaning of the act
- Best mode and enablement not sufficiently disclosed
- Issues related to priority date

- Disclosure regarding geographical source of the biological material involved is either not provided or wrongly mentioned in the complete specification
- Invention belongs to traditional knowledge which is in practice in public domain since ancient times.

Since the minimum time gap between date of publication and grant of patent is six months, so any person gets minimum assured six months to file a pre-grant opposition. Filed opposition should be supported with necessary evidence and a request for hearing if the person filing the opposition desires. Such opposition is taken into account during the generation of FER and is communicated to the applicant along with the FER. The applicant can provide his clarifications in writing within three months from the date of such notice, providing a copy to the opponent as well. The Controller takes into account all written arguments and those presented during hearing (if conducted) and depending upon the merit of the case takes a suitable decision. Controller may either reject the opposition, ask the applicant to amend the application or may reject the patent application itself by issuing an order under section 15 of the Indian Patents Act within one month of completion of all the proceedings related to hearing of both the parties involved. A pre-grant opposition cannot be filed after the grant of patent.

Sample copy of Form 7A

THE PATENTS ACT, 1970 (39 OF 1970)
AND THE PATENTS RULE, 2003

REPRESENTATION FOR OPPOSITION TO GRANT OF PATENT
[see rule 55]

1. State names, address and nationality.	**I/We, ... hereby give representation by way of opposition to the grant of patent of patent in respect of application no. .... Dated .... made by .... And published on...........**
2. State the grounds taken one after another	On the grounds ....
3. Complete address including postal index number/code and state along with telephone and fax number	My/Our address for service in India is ....
4. To be signed by the opponent or by his/her authorized registered patent agent	Signature

Contd...

5. Name and designation of the natural person who has signed	(.......................................)
To The Controller of patents The Patent office At .... (Delhi/Kolkata/Mumbai/Chennai)	

A schematic flowchart (figure 9.1) regarding the proceedings involved in pre-grant opposition is mentioned below for easy understanding of the readers,

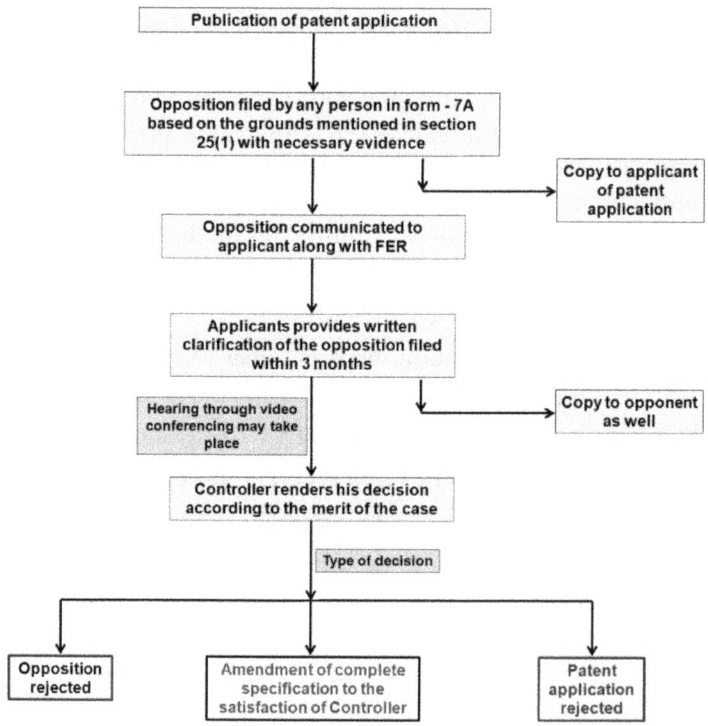

FIGURE 9.1 Proceedings of pre-grant opposition.

9.2 Post-Grant Opposition [Section 2(1)(t)]

Post-Grant opposition can be filed within one year from the grant of patent, one year to be counted from the date on which the intimation for grant of that particular patent was published in the official journal of the Indian patent office. Such opposition can be filed by an interested person

(person having relevance to that particular field of invention against which opposition is being filed) by applying in Form-7 and based on the grounds exclusively mentioned in Section 25(2) along with prescribed fee, a copy of the opposition document has to be provided by the opponent to the patentee. The grounds mentioned in Section 25(2) are as follows,

- Patent was wrongfully obtained from some other person
- The said invention as mentioned in the 'claims' of the complete specification has already been published before the filing of the application
- Invention had been in public use before the filing of the patent
- Subject matter involved, is not an invention within the true meaning of the act
- Best mode and enablement not sufficiently disclosed
- Patentee has provided false or not disclosed information to the Controller regarding foreign filing under Section 8
- For patent given on convention application, the said application may not have been filed within twelve months from the date of filing the basic application for the first time in some convention country
- Disclosure regarding geographical source of the biological material involved is either not provided or wrongly mentioned in the complete specification
- Invention belongs to traditional knowledge which is in practice in public domain since ancient times.

Upon receiving a post-grant opposition, the Controller constitutes a three-member (including the chairman) Opposition Board to examine the case under Section 25(3) of the Indian Patents Act. The examiner who has examined the patent application shall not be a member of the board. The Controller hands over the patent application along with the filed opposition including the replies given by either of the parties to the constituted Board for examining the merit of the case. Meanwhile, the Controller forwards the post-grant opposition to the patentee for filing suitable clarification along with evidence, which has to be filed within a period of two months, failing which the Controller may revoke the patent. A copy of the reply given by the patentee, also need to be communicated to the opponent. The opponent now can submit his reply to counter the clarification and evidence submitted by the patentee within one month. The Board shall submit its report to the Controller within three months (counted from the date on which all documents pertaining to the case was handed over to the Board) after duly studying the application, opposition filed and replies given by both the parties. The recommendations of the

Opposition Board along with a hearing notice is provided to both the parties. The hearing date has to be informed to both the parties at least ten days in advance. It depends upon both the parties whether they are willing to contest during the hearing, if so then they have to pay additional fees and inform the Controller in advance. The Controller may ask the Opposition Board to be present during the hearing. If either of the party wants to present any new evidence which was not filed earlier, then prior notice to the Controller and the other party has to be served at least five days prior to hearing. Upon completion of hearing, the Controller based on the merit of the case, evidences and arguments presented by both the parties and also taking into consideration the recommendations of the Board shall render a final decision. The final decision could be either rejection of opposition (patent continues) or revocation of patent or suitable amendment in the claims and specifications as well. A schematic representation of the sequence of events occurring in a post grant opposition is mentioned below.

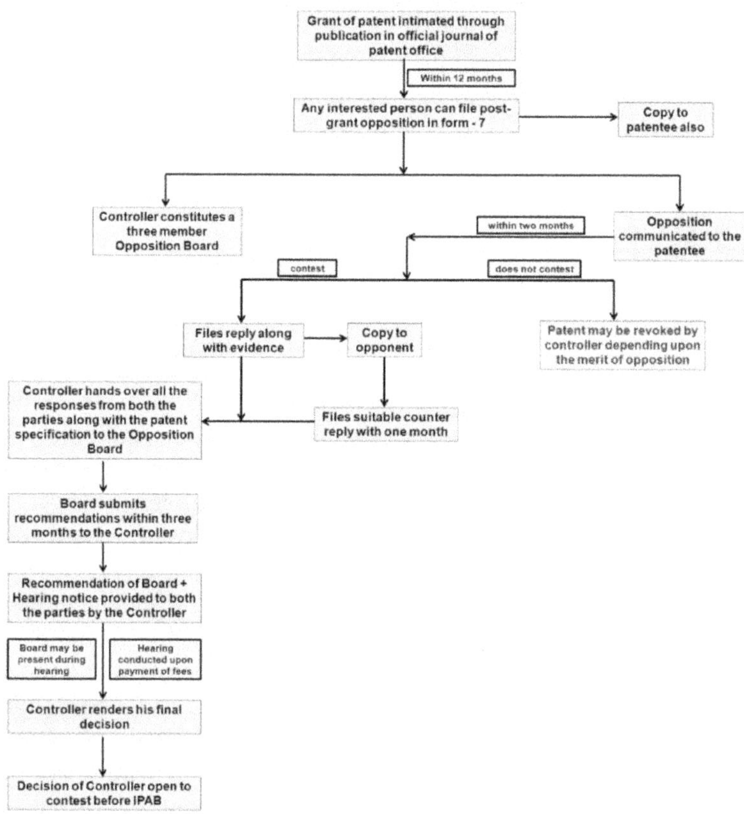

FIGURE 9.2 Proceedings of post-grant opposition.

Pre-grant opposition	Post-grant opposition
Can be filed by any person	Can be filed by an interested person who practices such relevant invention or has involvement with such field of invention
Infringement proceedings cannot be conducted during pre-grant opposition as the application is still under examination and no decision regarding the grant of patent has yet been taken	Infringement proceedings can be initiated as the patent has already been granted
Opposition Board may not be constituted	Three-member opposition Board is constituted
Less intense procedure as fewer formalities are involved	Intense procedure as more trials as in conventional court may be conducted
Fee not involved	Fee is required
If filed by any person, no remedy is available if the opposition is rejected by the Controller. However, if the opposition is allowed, the patentee can appeal before IPAB	Both opponent and patentee can appeal to IPAB
Hearing may not be necessary. Parties involved have to make a request for hearing	Hearing is generally conducted

A schematic representation (figure 9.3) of both pre and post-grant opposition have been mentioned below with time line for easy understanding of authors.

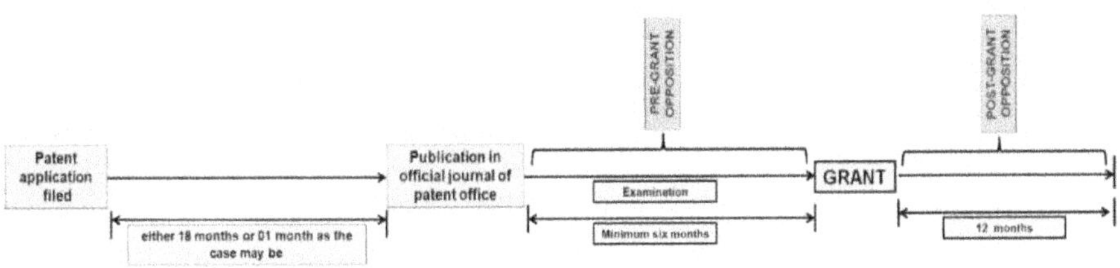

FIGURE 9.3 Time line for filing oppositions (pre and post grant oppositions).

All decisions of the Controller during both types of opposition are open to appeal before the IPAB by the applicant or patentee particularly when the opposition is allowed. Oppositions serves as a filter in removing frivolous inventions. Since patent provides exclusive monopoly to the patentee, so it is necessary that such monopoly is well tolerated by others, opposition in both forms are an indicative of such tolerance by the competitors. Opposition is more common in pharmaceutical inventions, where opposition is filed for any new drug by competitors who also have a similar product line. Such opposition pertaining to a new drug is more often based on proving the new drug as just a derivative and having a new property of an already known substance, is non-patentable under Section 3 of Indian Patents Act. The patentee shall try to defend his invention by proving that the derivative is absolutely chemically different from the parent molecule and provides a surprising synergistic effect. However, such opposition definitely delays the process of patent granting and increases the backlog cases with the patent office.

9.3 Revocation

Revocation of patent means cancellation of patent. Even though, patent is granted after meticulous examination of the application associated with a thorough search for novelty and inventive step, still there could be circumstances where questions can be raised about the integrity of the invention, which can even result in revocation of the patent. Most of the circumstances arise from counter claim associated with infringement suits. Any competitor may file a suit that a particular granted patent intrudes into their existing patent leading to battle of claims and counter claims in the form of court trials whose output could be cancellation or revocation of the patent. Below explained are the various circumstances which may lead to revocation of a patent,

1. ***Revocation instituted based on Section 65 & 99 and infringement suit***: Such revocations are ordered by IPAB and High Court. Central Government or any interested person (person having relevance to the field of invention) may file a petition for revocation of patent based on the reasons mentioned in Section 64 of Indian Patents Act, before the IPAB. Simultaneously a revocation can be ordered by High court as an outcome of the court proceedings of claim and counter claim of an infringement case. The various reasons which are highlighted in Section 64 of the Indian Patents Act are:
   - Issue related to priority claim where any of the claims mentioned in the granted patent happens to appear in a patent filed earlier to the previous patent in India
   - The patentee is not eligible for the patent and the invention was also obtained wrongfully from some other person

- The subject matter of the claim mentioned in the complete specification cannot be considered as an invention within the true meaning of the act
- Claimed invention lacks inventive step and hence is obvious
- Lack of sufficiency in disclosure which indicates that the best mode has not been revealed and neither the description enables a person skill in the art to carry out the invention without undue burden of unknown experiments
- Involvement of false representation
- Any of the claims mentioned, attracts provisions mentioned in Section 3 of Indian Patents Act which describes those inventions which are not patentable
- Inappropriate information or false information regarding foreign filing was provided by the applicant to the Controller under section 8 of Indian Patents Act
- Secrecy directions issued under Section 35 was contravened by the applicant
- Permission to amend the complete specification was falsely obtained
- False or inappropriate information regarding the source of any biological material mentioned in the complete specification was provided
- The invention is related to traditional knowledge or is being used by any indigenous community anywhere in the world before filing of the patent application.

If the Central Government files a petition that the patentee has failed to execute the patent (invention) as per the directions of the Central Government and the patent is not in a position to be used or exercised for the purpose desired by the Government, according to the provisions of Section 99, High Court if satisfied can order revocation of the said patent.

2. ***Revocation instituted due to relevance with atomic energy***: Such revocations are ordered by the Controller based on the directions obtained from Central Government. Any time after the grant of a patent, if Central Government is of the opinion that the said patented invention has relevance with atomic energy as per the provisions mentioned in the Atomic Energy Act, 1962, which was not previously observed during examination, may direct the Controller for revocation of the said patent because as per Section 4 of Indian Patents Act, no patent can be granted for inventions having relevance with atomic

energy. Nevertheless, the Controller may give opportunity to the patentee for amending the specifications so that the objection related to relevance with atomic energy can be rectified in order to save the patent.

3. ***Revocation instituted by Central Government on account of prejudicial inventions***: If the Central Government is of the opinion that a particular patented invention is harmfull (prejudicial) to the public or mischievous to the country, revocation may be ordered. However, opportunity shall be given to the patentee to be heard and if not satisfied, revocation order shall be passed post publication in Official Gazette.

4. ***Revocation instituted on account of non-working of patent with compulsory license***: If compulsory license has been granted to a patent and still even after two years from the grant of such license, the invention is still not commercialized within India or not affordable to the public in a reasonable price, revocation can be ordered. Even an interested person (must establish his interest in the field of invention) can institute a revocation on such ground. Decisions are generally rendered within one year from applying to Controller.

Case studies

Revocation case for non-compliance of section 8 (information to Controller regarding foreign filing carried out by applicant, such information has to be provided to the Controller till the grant of patent in India): Philips got a patent in 2007 regarding a technology associated with DVD. In 2012, Philips sued the proprietor Maj (Retd.) Sukesh Behl of Pearl Engineering for alleged infringement of their patented technology. Peral Engineering in defence filed a revocation case against Philips alleging that Philips did not comply with the provisions of Section 8, regarding providing information about foreign filing to the Controller within the prescribed 3 months' time limit at the end of every calendar year thus amounting to suppression of facts. Philips in return argued that, they did file all concerned information regarding a pending foreign filing but one of the legal team members mistakenly could not photocopy the back side of the last page containing some additional information related to the foreign filing. Such act was not intentional and occurred out of confusion or was mistakenly conducted and is not likely to cause any harm to the prosecution of such patent. Opponents' plea of revocation was rejected by the Court as there was no willful suppression of fact which was ascertained by the Court.

Hoffmann-La Roche Ltd. claimed in 2007 that it holds a granted Indian patent for 'Erlotinib Hydrochloride' which it is selling under the brand name 'TARCEVA'; which Cipla is infringing. Cipla also filed a counter claim. After a tough battle of court trials which initially was in Cipla's favour but finally the judgement came in favour of Roche and the patent of Roche was not revoked. The court observed that the Cipla's patent was on the product Polymorph B of the compound Erlotinib Hydrochloride. It was held by the judge that any process which involves producing Polymorph B of Erlotinib Hydrochloride have to go through the making of Erlotinib Hydrochloride first, in-fact it was further noted that Polymorph B results from re-crystallization of Erlotinib Hydrochloride. In light of the Section 3(d) of Indian Patents Act, court took into account that Polymorph B is not a 'new' product but a revisit of Erlotinib Hydrochloride and hence it was considered as an old product or rather a type of derivative of the original patented product Erlotinib Hydrochloride and since in the patent of Roche, Erlotinib Hydrochloride was completely disclosed so its derivative was also covered under the protection. Thus, the judgement resulted in the constitution of the infringement made by Cipla and Cipla was made to pay a cost of Rs 500,000. However, the court looking into public interest on the availability of the drug, did not grant a permanent order to stop the manufacturing by Cipla. This was a landmark judgement which further laid down guidelines for testing infringement cases. It was also said that when testing infringement, the infringing product and the marketed product (patented) is not to be compared but rather the claims mentioned in the patent is compared.

CHAPTER 10

Appeals

Appellate Board [Section 116, 117A(2)]

Two types of litigations can arise out of matters related to patent. The first being infringements cases where opponent claims encroachment of a granted patent into their existing one. Such cases are very common in pharmaceutical inventions and are dealt by High Court. In this regard, Delhi High Court has the maximum number of patent litigations registered with them. The other type of litigation arises when the applicant is not satisfied with the decisions rendered on their patent application or on their granted patent by the Controller or Central Government. The remedy available then is appeal before Intellectual Property Appellate Board (IPAB). The option of appeal available for patent litigations is explained below with the help of an illustration for the easy understanding of the readers.

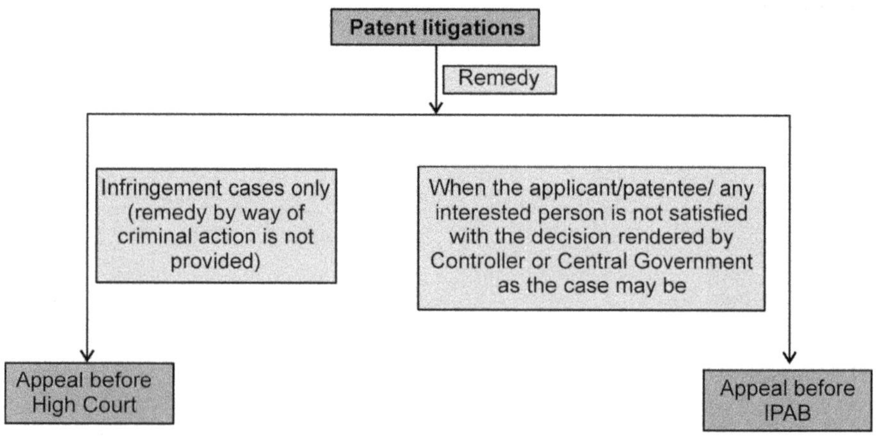

FIGURE 10.1 Appeal options in patent litigations.

Decisions of Controller and Central Government on any matter like patent refusal or revocation etc. may be appealed before competent authority by the applicant. In this regard, the Intellectual Property

Appellate Board (IPAB) was constituted on September 15, 2003 by a Gazette notification of the Central Government in the Ministry of Commerce and Industry. Initially IPAB was constituted with the objective that it would handle cases related to appeals against the decisions of the Registrar under the Trade Marks Act, 1999 and the Geographical Indications of Goods (Registration and Protection) Act, 1999. From April 2nd, 2007, IPAB was empowered to hear and adjudicate upon the appeals arising from the decisions, orders or directions made by the Controller related to patent cases under the Indian Patents Act. The Board is headquartered in Chennai with offices in Delhi, Kolkata and Ahmedabad as well. IPAB will attend to appeals arising from the decisions of the Controller or Central Government related to patent cases such as refusal of application, date related issues, anticipation, infringement, revocation, clerical errors correction in register of patent etc. However, orders passed by Central Government related to inventions having relevance with India's defence purposes, relevance of atomic energy, secrecy directions or revocation of inventions which are prejudicial to public are not appealable to IPAB. Also, those orders of the Controller, where an extension of time has been granted for some purpose under any provision of the Indian Patents Act is also not appealable. Every bench of IPAB has two members, one judicial member and one technical member who shall legally dispose of the appeal. Below mentioned are the list of those types of cases where appeal shall be heard by IPAB,

- Matters related to names of inventor
- Matters related to Patent of addition
- Disputes related to Divisional application
- Disputes related to priority date
- Matters related to alteration of entry in register of patent or any clerical errors
- Matters related to infringement
- Objections raised by applicant on matters related to refusal of patent application
- Disputes related to amendment of complete specification
- Matters related to revocation and restoration of lapsed patents
- Regarding surrender of patents
- Regarding substitution of applicants
- Matters related to compulsory licensing of patent

Applicant should file appeal before IPAB against the decision of the Controller on matters mentioned above in prescribed form, along with a certified copy of the decision of the Controller within three months from passing of the decision by the Controller/Central Government or within such further time limit as decided by IPAB. Prescribed fee ranging from Rs 5000 – 10000 may be required to be paid depending upon the category of the applicant (whether natural person or other than natural person). Controller also shall be heard during the hearing on matters relating to change in register of patent, matters related to refusal of patent grant for a particular application (either opposed or not) or in any other type of case as directed by the IPAB. However, with the permission of IPAB, instead of personal appearance, Controller can also provide his statement in writing and duly signed related to the proceedings, which shall also be treated as an evidence.

CHAPTER 11

Offences and Penalties

The different offences and penalties applicable for contravening the rules of Indian Patents Act are given below in tabular form for easy understanding of the readers,

TABLE 11.1 List of various offences along with penalties.

Nature of Offence	Punishment/Penalty	Section
If any applicant contravenes any provision related to secrecy directions (Section 35) or foreign filing (Section 39)	Imprisonment for maximum 2 years or/and fine	118
Any applicant causes false entry in any register maintained by the patent office by providing false information despite being aware of the fact that provided information is false	Imprisonment for maximum 2 years or/and fine	119
If any person makes a false claim of holding a patent or patent pending in India for any product which he is selling	Fine upto maximum of Rs. 100000	120
If any person uses any place of his business highlighting it to be a patent office or a center designated by Indian patent office	Imprisonment for maximum 6 months or/and fine	121
If any authorized person by central Government is using an invention for the purpose of government fails to furnish such information regarding the extent of use of the invention	Fine upto maximum of Rs. 1000000	122
Deliberately provides false information in Form-27 to the Controller regarding commercialization of a granted patent	Imprisonment for maximum 6 months or/and fine	122
Any person practicing without being a registered patent agent	Fine of Rs. 100000 for first offence and fine of Rs. 500000 for subsequent offence	123

If any of the above offence is made by any company, then every person who is responsible for conduct of business of the said company shall be subjected to suitable punishment. Nevertheless, such person can escape punishment on the grounds that the said offence was committed without his knowledge or he exercised his due powers to stop the offence, but could not, or the offence was committed due to negligence of any particular person.

CHAPTER 12

Forms, Fees and Sections

There are specified Forms available for making any kind of requisition to the Controller in respect to a particular patent application or patent. Such various Forms along with the purpose and fees to be paid are presented in a consolidated manner for easy understanding and remembrance of the readers. The below mentioned table presents all such Forms at a single glance.

TABLE 12.1 Consolidated information on various Forms along with time line and applicable fees [NP = natural person, SE = small entity alone or in combination with others, O = others alone or in combination with NP or SE]

Description	Form No.	Time frame for filing	Fee in INR (e-filing)			Fee in INR (physical-filing)		
			NP	SE	O	NP	SE	O
Application for patent	1	Immediate at the time of filing	1600	4000	8000	1750	4400	8800
Complete specification (30 pages and 10 claims allowed, for additional pages and claims extra charge levied)	2	Immediate at the time of filing	-	-	-	-	-	-
Information and undertaking regarding foreign filing as per the provisions mentioned in Section 8	3	Within 6 months from the date of filing the patent application						
Making request for seeking extension of time for payment of patent renewal under sections 53(2), and 142 (4)	4	Before expiry of the patent	480	1200	2400	530	1300	2600
Declaration as to inventorship	5	Within one month of filing complete specification	-	-	-	-	-	-
Application for substitution of applicants and may also be used for adding or removing an applicant from an Indian national phase patent application under PCT	6	Any time before grant	800	2000	4000	880	2200	4400

Table 12.1 *Contd...*

Description	Form No.	Time frame for filing	Fee in INR (e-filing)			Fee in INR (physical-filing)		
Filing pre-grant opposition	7A	Any time after publication of patent application but before grant of patent	-	-	-	-	-	-
Filing post-grant opposition	7	Within one year from the date of intimation of grant of patent in official journal of patent office	2400	6000	12000	2600	6600	13200
Mention of inventor as such in patent, Section 28(2), 28(3) or 28(7)	8	Before the grant of patent	800	2000	4000	880	2200	4400
Application for early publication (Section 11A-2)	9	At the time of filing or before the expiry of 18 months from the date of filing	2500	6250	12500	2750	6900	13750
Request for withdrawal of patent application	29	Any time after filing patent application and before grant. However, such request if filed for an application which is already under examination but FER has not yet been generated, 90% of the examination fee shall be refunded	-	-	-	-	-	-
Request for examination, Section 11(B)	18	At the time of filing patent application or within 48 months from the date of filing. If not filed within prescribe time limit, application is considered to be withdrawn.	4000	10000	20000	4400	11000	22000
Expedited examination	18A		8000	25000	60000	Paper filing of Form 18A is not permitted		

Table 12.1 *Contd...*

Description	Form No.	Time frame for filing	Fee in INR (e-filing)			Fee in INR (physical-filing)		
Amendment of patent granted to deceased person. If after the grant of patent, the patentee dies, the Controller upon satisfaction may amend the patent accordingly in the name of a legal representative of the patentee.	10	Anytime after grant of patent	2400	6000	12000	2650	6600	13200
Requisition made by co-owner of the patent to the Controller regarding sale/lease of the patent or regarding doing a particular thing as instructed on behalf of another co-owner due to the inability of the said co-owner to execute the given instructions by the Controller.	11	Any time after grant of patent	2400	6000	12000	2650	6600	13200
Requisition from the opponent upon wining the opposition case, to make the opposed patent amended in the name of the opponent (section 26(1)) or grant of patent to true and first inventor if the same was actually obtained by another by fraud (Section 52). In the latter case Appellate Board may permit the whole patent to be granted in the name of the true inventor by retaining the same patent number and date upon request from the petitioner.	12	Any time after grant of patent	2400	6000	12000	2650	6600	13200
Requisition for ammendement of patent application, complete specifications, priority date or any other document related to the application or patent, as the Controller thinks fit. However, such amendments are not possible if any opposition proceeding or infringement proceeding is ongoing or pending before the Appellate Board or the Hight court.	13	Any time before and after the grant of patent	Fee applicable before grant of patent					
			800	2000	4000	880	2200	4400
		Fee after grant of patent ⇒	1600	4000	8000	1750	4400	8800

Table 12.1 *Contd...*

Description	Form No.	Time frame for filing	Fee in INR (e-filing)			Fee in INR (physical-filing)		
Filing opposition for amendment of patent application, restoration of lapsed patent, surrender of patent	14	For amendment and surrender of patent, opposition may be filed within three months from the date of publication of such act in the official journal. For restoration of lapsed patent, opposition may be filed within two months from the date of publication in the official journal	2400	6000	12000	2650	6600	13200
Application for restoration of lapsed patent under Section 60	15	Within 18 months from the date on which the patent lapsed	2400	6000	12000	2650	6600	13200
Requisition for entry of title or notice of interest in the patent register in case any person becomes entitled to the patent by way of assignment, transmission of rights or by operation of law. Such application may be made either by the assignor or assignee	16	Any time after grant of patent and before expiry of patent	1600	4000	8000	1750	4400	8800
Application by any person for the grant of compulsory license for a particular granted patent, if the said patent could not be commercialized and the product could not be provided to the public at a reasonable price or the particular invention is not made to work within India	17	after the expiry of 3 years from the date of grant	2400	6000	12000	2650	6600	13200
Application for revocation of patent which has been granted compulsory license for non-working	19	After expiry of two years from the date of granting first compulsory license	2400	6000	12000	2650	6600	13200

Table 12.1 *Contd...*

Description	Form No.	Time frame for filing	Fee in INR (e-filing)			Fee in INR (physical-filing)		
Application for revision of terms and conditions settled by the Controller for compulsory licensing under Section 88(4)	20	After the person holding the compulsory license has worked on the invention at the commercial scale for not less than 12 months	2400	6000	12000	2650	6600	13200
Application by the patentee or any interested person deriving title or interest in the patent for termination of compulsory license which has been granted for the said license under Section 94	21	Anytime during the period of continuance of compulsory license, when the patentee is of the opinion that the circumstances which gave rise to the conditions of granting compulsory license, exists no more	2400	6000	12000	2650	6600	13200
Application for registering as a patent agent	22	After qualifying the examinations conducted by patent office	3200	--	--	3500	--	--
Application for restoration of name of any person removed from the register of patent agents on grounds of misrepresentation or the said person has been convicted of an offence and sentenced to imprisonment under Section 130	23	Within 2 months from the date of such removal	1600	--	--	1750	--	--
Application for review or setting aside any decision rendered by Controller on matters related to summoning, production of any document, examination of witness, awarding costs or any other matter under Section 77	24	To be applied by the applicant or opponent (whoever is aggrieved by the decision of the Controller) within 1 month from pronouncing such orders.	1600	4000	8000	1750	4400	8800

Table 12.1 *Contd...*

Description	Form No.	Time frame for filing	Fee in INR (e-filing)		Fee in INR (physical-filing)			
To apply for FFL (foreign filing license) under section 39	25	When the applicant is not willing to file an Indian patent application for the said invention, in such case to procced directly for foreign filing FFL has to be obtained by applying in Form 25	1600	4000	8000	1750	4400	8800
For providing power of authority to a patent agent by an applicant to handle	26	Whenever the applicant desires to hire a patent agent	--	--	--	--	--	--
Statement regarding commercialization of a patented invention	27	Within 2 months when asked by the Controller to furnish such information regarding the patented invention	--	--	--	--	--	--
For claiming fee reduction on account of being a small entity or startup	28	To be submitted with every document which is associated with submission of fee	--	--	--	--	--	--
For making miscellaneous requisition when no other form is specified	30	As the case may be						

Important Sections

Sections	Description
6	Persons who are entitled to apply for patent application
3	Inventions which are not patentable
8	Information and undertaking regarding foreign filing
16, 74	Jurisdiction – in-order to decide at which patent office the applicant should apply for patent
7, 16, 54, 135	Explains different types of patent such as ordinary patent application, convention application, PCT national phase application, divisional application, patent of addition
7	Filing of patent application (documents required)
35	Secrecy directions
4	Inventions related to atomic energy cannot be patented
11A 11B	Publication of patent application including early publication and provision for withdrawal of patent application Request for examination
9	Provision regarding provisional and complete specification
10 10(4) 10(4A) 10(4) 10(5)	Contents of specifications Contents of complete specification National phase application Claims Unity of Invention
16	Divisional application
54,55	Patent of addition
2(1)(j) 2(1)(ac)	Novelty and Inventive step Industrial applicability
133-138	Convention application
12	Examination of application
13	Search for anticipation by previous publication or prior claiming
25	Opposition to a patent
29-31	Anticipation and not anticipation
39	Rules of foreign filing, no Indian resident can apply for foreign filing without prior permission from Indian patent office
43	Grant of patents
60-62	Associated with restoration of lapsed patents
63	Surrender of patents
64	Revocation of patents
67	Register of patents and particular's to be entered
78	Power of Controller to correct clerical errors in the register of patents
84,86,87,88,89, 90,91,92,94	Compulsory licenses (grant procedure, terms, termination)

CHAPTER 13

Foreign Filing

13.1 Rules of Filing Patent Application by an Indian Resident in a Foreign Country

The two routes available for an applicant or inventor residing in India for filing a foreign patent application is either through a convention application in any convention country or filing an international application under PCT. However, Section 39 of Indian Patents Act clearly sets provision for restricting any person residing in India to file a foreign patent application without obtaining a prior approval from the Indian patent office in the form of Foreign Filing License (FFL). The options available to a person residing in India and willing to file a foreign patent application are,

- Apply for an Indian patent first, and then wait for a minimum period of six weeks before filing the application in foreign country. If no objections or secrecy directions are received within six weeks of Indian filing, the applicant can then proceed for foreign filing in the country he desires. No approval from Indian patent office is now required once a period of six weeks have been completed after filing an Indian application, provided no secrecy directions or other objections are imposed in the said period
- If an applicant wishes to directly file a foreign application without filing an Indian application, may be because the product coming out of the said invention is not likely to be used in India as there exist no market segment for such products, or such inventions are not patentable in India, in such circumstance the applicant shall need to apply for a FFL from the India patent office. FFL is a written consent whereby, Indian patent office waives the requirement of filing an Indian application first before going for a foreign filing. Even though, an Indian application has been filed, but the applicant is not willing to wait for six weeks, FFL is also required in such case.

A schematic diagram representing the entire scenario of how to proceed for foreign filing by an Indian resident is given below for easy understanding of the readers,

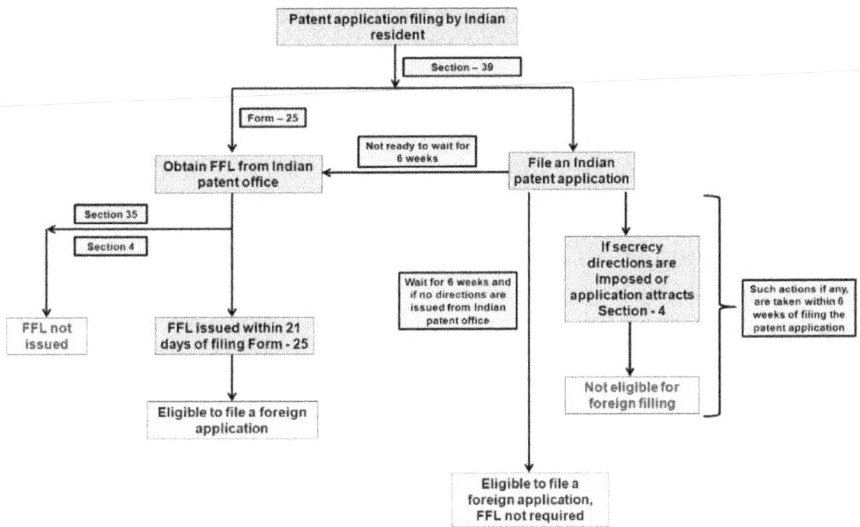

FIGURE 13.1 Procedure for foreign filing by an Indian resident.

Through such provisions mentioned under Section 39 of Indian Patents Act, Government of India keeps a strict vigil on all innovations going out of India. This is necessary because, if any invention pertaining to India's defence purposes (like innovations associated with explosives or radar systems etc.) goes out of the country, may pose a serious threat to India's defence and national security. Through granting FFL, Government provides a green signal to the applicant for foreign filing and also the Government is assured that the said invention is no threat to the country's national security. When an Indian application is filed first, preliminary screening of all such filed application is likely to be completed within the first six weeks and if any relevance is found to India's defence purposes, secrecy directions shall be imposed. Provisions under Section 4 (atomic energy relevance) shall also be imposed if such relevance is found. In such circumstances, the applicant shall be intimated within six weeks and no foreign filing shall be possible, even the publication of the application in India is also not possible, until suitable clearance from Central Government is obtained. Nevertheless, if the applicant hears nothing from the India patent office within the first six weeks, he is good to go for foreign filing, FFL shall not be required then. For obtaining a FFL, applicant has to apply in Form 25, the Controller shall render his decision in such matters except to those cases having relevance to India's defence and atomic energy, within 21 days of filing Form 25. Below mentioned are the basic documentation required for obtaining a FFL,

- Form-25
- Brief write up of the invention, complete specification is not required at this stage
- Details of all inventors involved
- Name of the foreign country where the applicants wish to file patent application with justification
- Assignee, if any
- Power of attorney, in case the services of any authorized patent agent is being hired by the applicants
- Form-28, if the applicant is a Small Entity.

<table>
<tr><td colspan="2">Sample copy of Form-25

FORM 25
THE PATENTS ACT, 1970
(39 OF 1970)
&
The Patents Rules, 2003
REQUEST FOR PERMISSION FOR MAKING PATENT APPLICATION OUTSIDE INDIA
[See Section 39 and Rule 71(1)]</td></tr>
<tr><td>1. State the title of the invention</td><td>I am/We are in possession of an invention for....................
I/We have made an application for the grant of a patent for the said invention, its number being No of ...... Dated ....
OR
I/We hereby attach the brief description of the invention</td></tr>
<tr><td>2. Name and address of the person(s)</td><td>I/We intend to make application(s) alone/jointly with .... for the same/substantially same invention for patent in the following country/countries/convention countries, namely: -
......................................</td></tr>
</table>

Contd.....

Name and address of the assignee	I/we declare that the rights in the application(s) has/have been assigned to .... I/We request that I/We may be granted permission to make application(s) for the said invention in the said country/countries. The reasons for making this application, are as follows: - .... The facts and matters stated above are true to the best of my/our knowledge, information and belief. Dated this .... Day of .... 20 .... Signature ....
3. To be signed by applicants(s) or authorized patent agent	To The Controller of patents The Patent office, At .... (Delhi, Kolkata, Mumbai, Chennai)
[Note – (a) strike out whichever is not applicable, (b) For fee: See First schedule]	

Any contravention of Section 39, shall attract imprisonment extendable upto two years or with fine, or may be both. However, even after carrying out foreign filing with FFL from Indian patent office, necessary information should be passed on to the controller regarding all such foreign filing done by the applicant till the grant of patent in India to comply with Section 8 of Indian Patents Act.

13.2 Convention Application

Any application which is filed in the home country first (need to be a convention country) or in any convention country and then subsequently filed in any of the convention country or countries within 12 months of the basic filing, the advantage of priority date is provided for subsequent filings. The application which is filed first in the home country or any convention country is known as the basic application; whose priority date is protected, if subsequent filing of the same invention in other convention countries is undertaken within 12 months of basic filing. The priority date applicable for the basic filing is also considered for the subsequent filing of the same invention in the above-mentioned case. Convention countries are those countries which have agreed upon to implement the proceedings of Paris Convention and are also known as member states. The concept of convention application was decided to be implemented in Paris Convention 1883. India became a convention country in 1998. The basic documentation required for filing a convention application in India are,

- Complete specification along with claims and abstract
- The date and the name of the convention country in which the basic application was made first
- Statement from applicant indicating that no any application related to the said invention is made in any convention country before the priority date claimed
- Priority document (certified copy) is to be submitted. If priority document is in any language other than English, a verified copy of its English translation shall be provided

A schematic diagram depicting the concept of Convention application is given below for easy understanding of the readers,

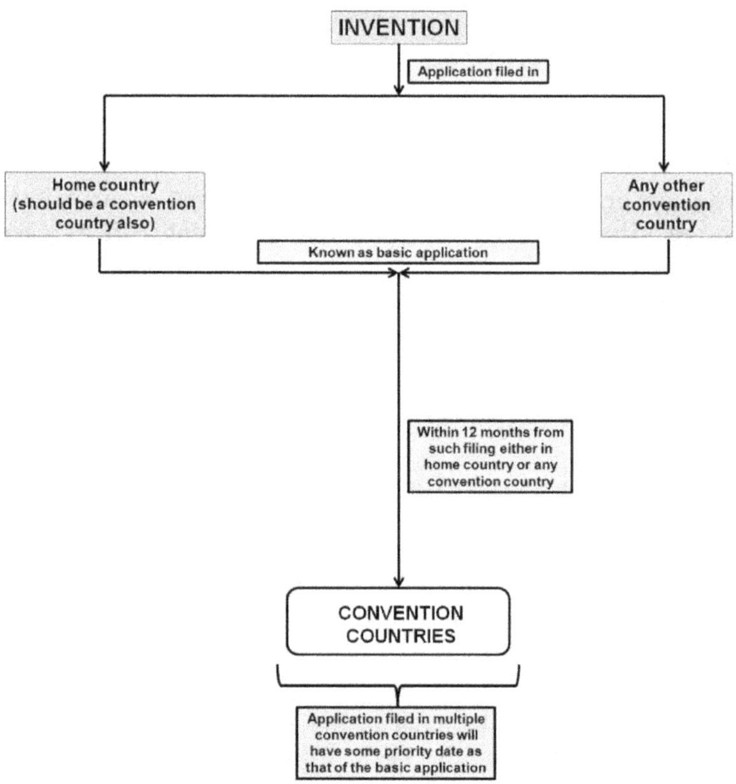

FIGURE 13.2 Illustrative representation of convention application concept.

Convention applications are also granted for twenty years (in India). A convention application may be post-dated but not beyond the date which is out of the 12 months window provided for filing convention application.

13.3 International Application under Patent Cooperation Treaty (PCT)

Patent Cooperation Treaty (1970) is an international treaty which is administered by WIPO and related to filing international patent applications. The treaty provides a single common window to all member countries (contracting states) for filing a single international application under a single filing mechanism with protection of priority date to enter into national phase of all designated contracting states. In this filing mechanism described under PCT procedure, the applicant preferably files the patent application for the first time (basic application) at his home country (must be a member of PCT) and then gets 12 months' time to file a single international application at the designated receiving office or at the WIPO head office in Geneva. The applicant need not apply individually in foreign countries for patent filing in this case as PCT is a single shot application for filing in respective member countries. The greatest advantage that PCT system offers is protection of priority date, provided the PCT application is filed within 12 months of filing the basic application. Once patent is granted at different designated countries under PCT, the protection shall begin from the date of filing the basic application. Thus, an applicant gets 12 months buffer time after filing the basic application preferably in the home country to arrange for revenue to meet the expenditures associated with PCT filing and also gets sufficient time to decide which PCT member countries to target for filing at a later stage. However, it must be clear to the readers that there is nothing called international patent. PCT is just a mutually agreed route to simplify international patent filing, consented by PCT member countries. Through this PCT route which is administered by WIPO, the international application after a certain time period and after certain processing enters into the national phase of respective PCT member countries as designated by the applicant in his PCT application. However, when the application enters the PCT member countries, applicant by that time gets sufficient opportunity to understand the patentability scope of his invention and also gets opportunity to amend the application, in light of the prior art search as revealed during the processing stage. Thus, the application is refined and its patentability scope is enhanced. All the member countries shall treat this incoming PCT application in the same way as if it is a patent application filed by their own nationals, and shall be given the same priority as given to their own national patent application. At this stage the applicant has to fulfil all the document related formalities of that particular country. Most often the PCT international application which was initially filed by the applicant serves the purpose because it is very exhaustive and almost fulfils the paper work of all member countries in a single shot. Nevertheless, some member countries may require translation in their own national language or may even need certain additional documents which the applicant has to arrange in prescribed time. Applicant has to also pay the fees applicable for each PCT member country where the PCT international application has been routed. The decision on granting the patent by a particular PCT country shall be based on the national patent laws of that particular country. WIPO does not administer any common international law for granting patent to PCT applications. It is highly possible that the same application may be granted patent in one PCT member country, but at the same time may get rejected in another PCT member country, all depends on the existing patent laws of respective PCT member countries. However, decision of grant of patent or rejection by one PCT member country shall not affect the decision-making process of another PCT member country and each of the countries shall grant or reject an application independently based on their existing national patent laws. But one thing is common in this route that the patent if granted, protection starts from the date of filing the basic application. The maximum time allowed for filing a PCT application from the date of filing a basic application is 12 months. The stages involved in PCT filing is highlighted below for a step by step understanding of the readers,

1. Filing of an international PCT application at the regional office or directly with the WIPO head office at Geneva (mandatory step). Filing has to be done within 12 months of filing the basic application in any PCT member country.
2. Handling and processing of filed application by internationally designated authorities in terms of establishing a search report and producing a written opinion on the patentability of the invention and transmittal of such report to WIPO (mandatory step).
3. If the applicant desires, can make amendment to the application in light of the search report produced (optional).
4. Publication of the application by WIPO on PATENTSCOPE (database which provides access to the applications filed under PCT) (mandatory step).
5. Supplementary international search followed by international preliminary examination by an International Preliminary Examining Authority (optional).

6. By the end of 30/31 months from the priority date, the PCT application finally enters into the respective PCT member country as designated by the applicant during filing of the PCT application. This stage is known as National Phase, where each respective country shall evaluate the application according to the existing patent laws of that particular country and then decide on granting or rejecting the patent application. Noteworthy, to mention that at the national stage, the applicant shall have to fulfil the additional requirements in terms of documents and fees applicable for each member country where the PCT application has entered.

A PCT international application may be submitted at any of the four patent offices of India or directly with the International Bureau of WIPO. Offices which are authorized to receive PCT applications are known as Receiving Office (RO). Application can be submitted both through online (using e-PCT module) and offline mode (application copy shall be submitted in triplicate). Form number PCT/RO/101 (which can be downloaded from WIPO website) has to be submitted in triplicate for offline submission along with descriptions, claims, abstracts and drawings (if any). The applicant needs to pay three kind of fees at this stage namely, Transmittal fee (for transmitting the PCT application to WIPO and other authorities for the purpose of search), International filling fee and Search fee, either at the time of application or within one month from the date of receipt of PCT application by the RO. However, if PCT application is filed by a natural person, provision for providing 90% reduction in international filing fee exist. The transmittal fee for Indian applicant is Rs 17600 for paper filing, no fee is required in case of e-filing mode. International filing fee for an Indian applicant is USD 1453 for 30 sheets, beyond which USD 16 is charged per sheet. The RO upon receipt of the application performs the following checks,

- Nationality of the applicant (must be an Indian national for using Indian patent office as RO for PCT applications). In case of involvement of multination applicant, at-least one of the applicants must be of India national to obtain the right to use Indian patent offices as RO. However, if such criteria are not met, then the international application is refereed to International Bureau, WIPO which being the headquarter is eligible to receive all PCT applications from all member countries.
- The language of PCT application where India is the RO, shall be either in English or Hindi.
- The application filed, must be clearly demarcated by the applicant as PCT international application.

- Indication regarding which contracting state the applicant wants to enter through PCT route after initial processing must be provided.
- If appropriate fees have been paid.
- Indication regarding the choice of International Search Authority (ISA). Every member country has a designated list of ISA from whom one can assign a particular ISA to carry out the search and generate a written opinion.
- Indication regarding choice of International Preliminary Examination Authority (IPEA) (optional).

The international filing date is considered as the actual filing date in each country, where the applicant wants to enter via the PCT route. Nevertheless, if the application gets granted for patent in any member country, the date of protection shall begin from the filing date of basic application, provided subsequent filing of international application was made within 12 months. Upon completion of preliminary checks, RO retains one copy and marks it as 'Home Copy', directs one copy to the International Bureau, WIPO as 'Record Copy' and the last copy to the designated International Searching Authority (ISA) naming it as 'Search Copy'.

Every application is subjected to international search by ISA which has been designated by the applicant at the time of filing the application. For Indian applicants the following ISAs are available,

- Indian Patent Office (IN)
- Australian Patent Office (AU)
- Austrian Patent Office (AT)
- European Patent Office (EP)
- The State Intellectual Property Office of The People's Republic of China (CN)
- United States Patent & Trademark Office (US)
- Swedish Patent and Registration Office (SE).

The search fee charged by Indian Patent Office is INR 2500 for any natural person and INR 10000 for others. Only few patent offices of the world have been designated as ISA and IPEA and in this regard the Delhi branch of the Indian Patent Office started functioning as ISA/ISEA from 15th October, 2013. The designated ISA performs the search to trace any relevant prior art both in the form of patent and technical literature available in the public domain, which is likely to influence the patentability aspect of the invention. A written opinion is made by the said ISA on the patentability of the invention. The ISA establishes the said report along with written opinion within a period of three months from the date of receipt of 'Search Copy', or within nine months from the date of priority, whichever is later. The ISA can also deny search of the application and generation of written opinion, if the international application fails to comply with the requirements prescribed under the treaty to conduct a meaningful search. Such event is also possible, if the international application does not reflect 'Unity of Invention'. In such cases, notice is sent to the applicant regarding the same. The PCT international application along with search report and written opinion is published online in PATENTSCOPE (https://patentscope.wipo.int/search/en/search.jsf) which is WIPO's global database for PCT applications, within 18 months from the priority date. PATENTSCOPE is available for public inspection. In light of the above fact, ISA produces the search report and written opinion within 16 months from the priority date, which is before the publication of the international application. Based on the written opinion issued by ISA, the applicant gets an opportunity to make suitable amendments to increase the patentability scope of the invention. Such amendments shall be communicated to the WIPO before publication of the application in PATENTSCOPE. It may be noted that the search report generated by ISA in not binding on the applicant.

The next step in PCT processing is International Preliminary Examination (IPE), which is an optional procedure. If interested, applicant may apply with one of the designated international patent offices as mentioned above along with Form PCT/IPEA/401. Fees required for IPE is 2500 for natural person and 10000 for others if the earlier search report and written opinion was generated by the Indian Office. However, if the search report was generated by another authorized International Patent Office, the fees shall be 3000 and 12000 for natural person and others, respectively. Nevertheless, if IPE is not opted by the applicant, the search report along with the written opinion of ISA is published with the application. International preliminary examination is a kind of mock examination before the application enters the PCT member countries as designated by the applicant during filing of the international application. Such examination provides an additional search report which is a kind of a second opinion which shall further help in eliminating the hurdles for patenting the invention. The request for IPE has to be filed by the applicant within 22 months from the priority date or within 3 months of receiving the search report along with the written opinion of ISA, whichever date is later. The IPEA establishes the report within 22 months from the priority date or 06 months from the start of IPE. Based on the IPEA report, applicant may amend the application which shall make the application more robust thereby, decreasing rejection chances when the application enters the PCT member countries as the application has been by then refined twice in light of the already existing prior art.

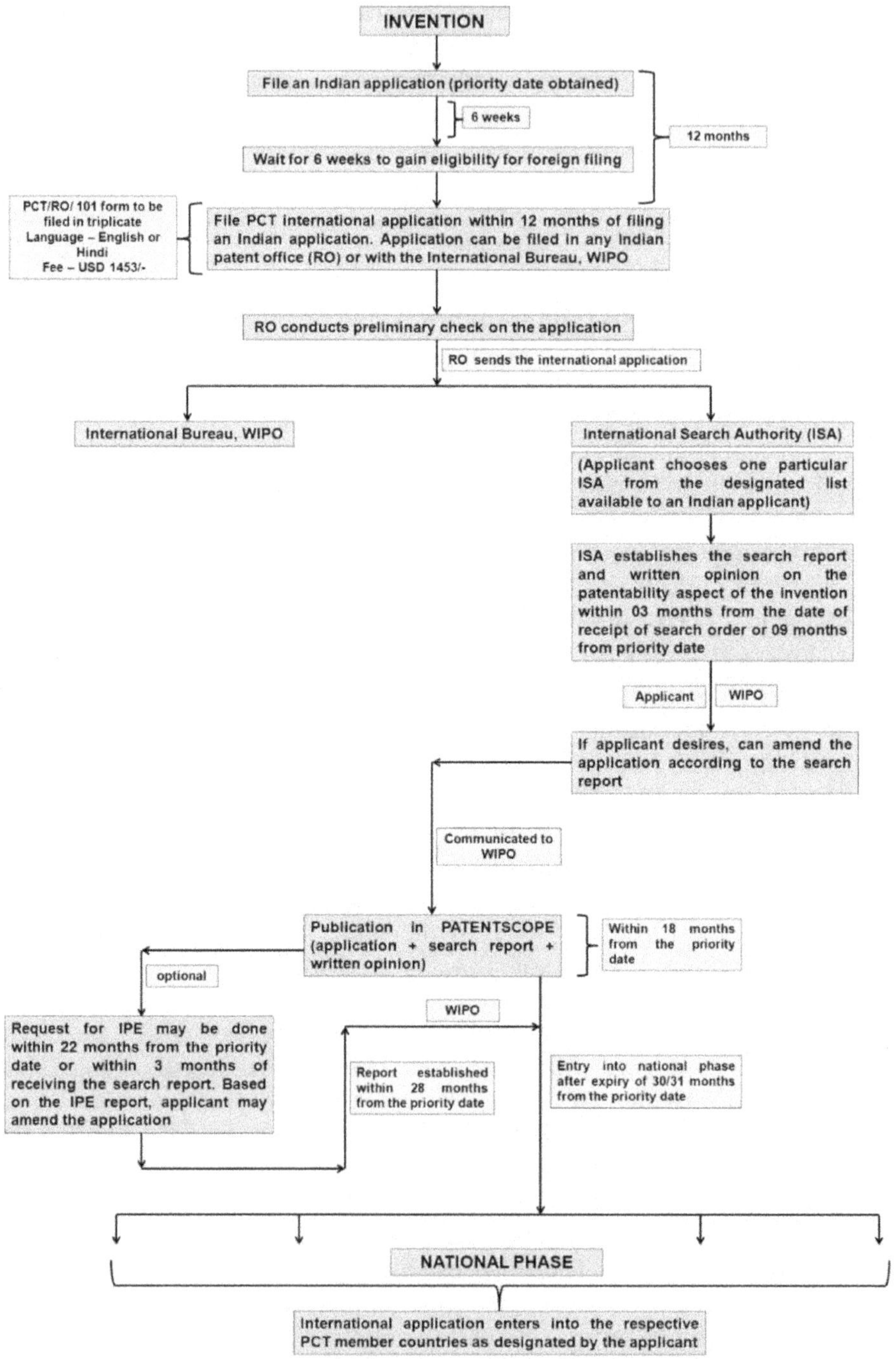

FIGURE 13.3 Steps in PCT filing.

The final stage in PCT processing is entry of the international application in the PCT member countries as designated by the applicant during filing of the international application. This phase, when the PCT international application enters the respective PCT member countries is known as National Phase which takes place within 30/31 months from the priority date. Indian patent law provides a time span of 31 months from the priority date for entry of PCT international application into India. The said time period of 30/31 months can be extended depending upon the national patent laws of respective PCT member countries. An illustrative explanation of the different steps involved in PCT filing is given in Fig. 13.3, in the form of a flowchart for easy understanding of the readers.

During the national phase, the applicant has to file a national application as per the requirements of the respective PCT member countries, which he has chosen to enter for seeking protection of his invention. In most of the cases as explained earlier, the PCT international application itself serves the purpose, but the applicant may have to fulfil requirements of additional documents as per the norms of the patent office of each respective country. The applicant also needs to pay fees associated with patent processing for each country where the international application enters. For example, any application entering India through PCT route, applicant needs to file Form-1 which is a basic patent application form. The Indian Patent Office where the national phase application has to be filed depends on the address of service provided in the Form-1, that particular address shall decide the jurisdiction. The international application shall serve as Form-2 which indicates complete specification. The application now directly moves to examination provided the applicant files Form-18 and pays requisite fee for examination. Rest of the procedure is same as followed for a normal Indian patent application filed in India. However, if the international patent application was filed in some other language other than English, the Indian office shall ask for a certified translated copy of the same. Priority document also needs to be submitted during the national phase so that the priority date can be established. The decision to reject or grant the patent shall now be made according to Indian Patents Act, for an application entering India through PCT route, WIPO shall have no say in this regard.

Withdrawing the international application is open to the applicant anytime before the expiry of 30 months from priority date. The applicant has to give a notice expressing his desire to withdraw the application either to the RO or to the International Bureau, WIPO. Publication of the application shall not take place if the withdrawal reaches WIPO before technical preparations required for publishing the application in

PATENSCOPE. The other types of withdrawal which the applicant may request for are as follows,

- The applicant specifies the contracting states (PCT member countries) which he desires to enter for protecting the said invention, at the time of PCT filing of the international application. At any given time before the expiry of thirty months from the priority date, the applicant may withdraw any of the contracting states which he has designated at the time of filing the application. However, withdrawing of all member countries shall eventually lead to withdrawal of the application, because under such circumstances the application shall have no PCT member country to enter after thirty months as national phase.
- The applicant may apply for withdrawal of priority claim, any time before the expiry of thirty months from the priority date. If such withdrawal results in change of priority date, then all computation regarding time line shall now be computed from the changed priority date
- Applicant may place a request for withdrawal of supplementary search request (search carried out during IPE) which is a optional procedure. In case the applicant has placed a request for IPE, then an additional search is carried out by IPEA as a second opinion. Withdrawal of such request can be made before the search report is established and communicated to the applicant and to the International Bureau, WIPO.

CHAPTER 14

Patent Laws Relating to Traditional Knowledge and Role of TKDL

India has a rich heritage of '**Traditional Knowledge**' in the form of Ayurveda, Unani, Siddha etc. which are being practiced since ancient times. Such knowledge is documented in ancient books and is also passed from one generation to another. Such subject matter which is already existing in public domain since ancient times and is in practice cannot be patented. But still there have been instances where Indian Patent Office have granted patents on the use of traditional knowledge of India. Patents have also been granted on various inventions having association with biological resources acquired from India. Patents in foreign countries have also been granted on this subject matter. However, those were the things of the past, as now with the birth of TKDL; the current scenario has changed globally. India has now made sufficient legal provision in protection of traditional knowledge and biological resources, clearly based on the fact that such knowledge has been prevailing in the country since ancient times and now also exists in digitally documented form (TKDL) in different foreign languages and accessible to different countries. India has successfully negotiated with other International Patent Offices (USPTO, EPO etc.) regarding using TKDL as an authenticated source for evaluating the novelty and inventive step of patent applications having relevance with traditional knowledge. Henceforth, such countries shall search the TKDL database for novelty and inventive step for any such application.

The Receipt, Sorting & Distribution (RECS) section of the patent office shall screen all documents to identify all those applications which have any relevance with traditional knowledge. Such application shall be given the tag of 'Traditional Knowledge' by RECS section so that the application can be examined by a dedicated group of examiners having expertise in handling inventions associated with traditional knowledge. Patent examiners are divided into specific groups operating under a team leader. Such team leader within a group shall act as the Controller in taking specific decisions. Various team leaders for different groups like 'chemistry, pharmaceutical's, agrochemicals, biotechnology, food' etc. should identify few examiners in the group who can be made dedicated for handling inventions having relevance with traditional knowledge. For any inventions related to traditional knowledge, examiners mandatorily must search for anticipation in TKDL or other similar databases. If any reference for the invention is found in such databases, citation of the same must be included in the FER.

The following golden principles must be taken into consideration for the assessment of novelty and inventive step for evaluating any application having association with traditional knowledge.

1. If the subject matter of the claims has relation to extracts of plant material containing unidentified active ingredients (phytoconstituents), such type of claims cannot be considered to be novel, when the use of such plants is already practiced in the society as a part of knowledge available through traditional knowledge. Even if, some alkaloids or active ingredient are isolated from the plant material and subsequently characterized, which do not form a part of the teaching available from traditional knowledge, still such claims cannot be said to have an inventive step which is a prerequisite for patent. Since the available teachings from traditional knowledge can easily motivate a person skilled in the art to isolate the active ingredients such as alkaloids, glycoside, phenolics etc.

   Invention: Plant 'A' (roots) - extract is claimed to be effective in management of diabetes

   Prior art: Plant 'A' (leaves) – reported for management of diabetes, but there are no reports of any active ingredient identified

   Analysis: (a) Since the plant 'A' already finds use in traditional knowledge system, irrespective of any part used, so any person skilled in the art can get motivated and using common logical thinking can take up the said plant for extract preparation – thus there involves no inventive step because such invention can be achieved through logical systematic thinking. In light of the teachings available for leaves of plant 'A', any person skilled in the art is likely to try out other parts for extract preparation for the management of diabetes, hence the invention becomes very obvious. (b) The said plant is already in use in the domain and so is the active ingredient which is already present in the plant and whenever the extract is administered as per the teachings of traditional knowledge, the said active ingredient was also used along with the extract, even though its identity was unknown but it still existed in the said extract. The plant owes its activity because of the presence of such active ingredient either alone or in combination with other phytoconstituents. Therefore, the prior art (teachings available from traditional knowledge) motivates the person skilled in the art to isolate and establish the identity of the active ingredient which is likely to have the same therapeutic effect. Hence isolation of such active ingredients and characterizing them cannot be considered to have an inventive step in light of the teachings reflected from traditional knowledge.

2. Combining plants whose therapeutic effects are already known with other multiple plants, understood to have being known for treating the same disease, is considered to be an obvious invention lacking inventive step.

   Invention:

   Plant A
Plant B
Plant C } combination is being claimed for the treatment of wound healing

   Prior art: Reveals that plants A, B and C are independently reported for the treatment of wound healing.

   Analysis: Since all the three plants (A, B and C) are already used separately, so its obvious that their combined effect shall also likely show the same activity and may also be improved in nature which just indicates cumulative aggregation of the individual properties of the participating components (plants A, B and C).

3. If an ingredient (plant material/active ingredient) is already known for the treatment of a particular disease, then it can be easily assumed that any combination product comprising of the said ingredient would be effective for the treatment of that particular disease.

   Invention:

   Plant A
Plant B
Plant C } this combination has been found effective for the management of diabetes

   Prior art: Discloses that only plant 'B' has been used in the management of diabetes.

   Analysis: Since plant 'B' has already been reported alone for treatment of diabetes, so if it is used in combination with other plants (not reported for management of diabetes), then it becomes a clear assumption that the combination product is likely to exhibit antidiabetic property because of the presence of plant B.

4. Findings which reveal the optimum working ranges of traditionally known ingredients by routine experimentation is not considered to be inventive.

   Invention:

   5-10% of extract of plant A
   15-20% extract of plant B
   60-70% extract of plant C
   } Formulation comprising of the prescribed combination used for the treatment of ulcer

   Prior art: Reveals the use of extracts of plant A or B or C for the treatment of ulcer.

   Analysis: even though TKDL might not have evidence for the use of the said plants in the prescribed composition or the exact combination of all the three mentioned plants may not be available from the teachings of traditional knowledge, but decision regarding the exact composition by a person skilled in the art can be reached through routine optimization and experimentation, hence lacks inventive step.

5. In case where multiple ingredients are involved and all are known to possess the same therapeutic effect according to the teachings of traditional knowledge, in such case taking out one particular ingredient from the composition cannot be undertaken as an invention.

   Invention:

   Extract from Plant A ---- claims use of Plant 'A' for treatment of inflammation.

   Prior art: Reveals the use of a particular combination of Plant 'A' + Plant 'B' + Plant 'C' for the treatment of inflammation.

   Analysis: Since Plant 'A' in combination with other Plants 'B' and 'C' is already in use for the treatment of inflammation, so it is not surprising that any person skilled in the art can be easily motivated to try out Plant 'A'alone which does not require exercising any inventive skills. The decision can be easily taken based on logical common sense.

6. If certain individual ingredients (plants or phytoconstituents) are already known for the treatment of a particular disease as per the teachings from TKDL, then it becomes obvious that a combination product comprising of such plants with other known plants having the same known therapeutic effect would likely be more effective than each of the medicinal plants when used separately. It is a clear representation of aggregation of properties causing an additive effect.

Invention:

Plant A
Plant B
Plant C

} Composition comprising of these plants for treatment of wound (wound healing property)

Prior art: Reveals the use of all said plants for the treatment of wound separately. The combination claimed is not mentioned in TKDL.

Analysis: Since plants A, B and C all are separately used for the purpose of wound healing, so it is obvious that their combination is likely to be better than when each of them is used alone. Hence, there involves no inventive step.

Even though, the rules for patenting any invention which has involvement of traditional knowledge are very stringent but still, this is not the end of research for natural product researchers. However, natural product researchers need to be very critical in their thinking and research outcome on the following points, which if presented well; can go in favour of the researcher with respect to obtaining a patent for any invention which involves traditional knowledge,

- Research should clearly indicate a synergistic effect or a surprising effect. Exhibition of cumulative aggregation of properties of the ingredients involved shall go against the researcher in terms of obtaining a patent. A synergistic effect or a surprising effect is something which is beyond and much more than a simple cumulative effect of the ingredients involved and is also considered beyond the thinking of a person with ordinary skills.
- Researchers should show that the results have been obtained through a battery of well-designed exhaustive experimentation and is not just an outcome of some trial-and-error procedures conducted through routine experimentation. The complexity involved in the work should be clearly visible. The researchers than can defend, that any person with ordinary skill in the art cannot undertake such complexity and such heavy experimentation load is also beyond the capacity of a person with ordinary skills. Such arguments may reflect an inventive step in the said invention.
- Researchers should indicate that a long-felt need was fulfilled through this particular research.
- Researchers should show significant increase in yield or output from the experimental results which could not have been achieved through traditional experimental approach.

CHAPTER 15

Patent Term Extension

Patent term extension refers to extending the patent protection for a particular invention beyond the standard duration of 20 years. However, this patent term extension is not applicable for all types of inventions. In India there is no such provision of patent term extension and patent protection is granted for standard duration of 20 years only. However, the question of why patent term extension is required, arises because of the fact that for pharmaceutical products and medical devices or such other chemicals which may be consumed by humans/animals, regulatory approval from the regulatory authorities of that particular country is required. Such approval is extremely time consuming and requires extensive data with special emphasis to clinical data. Patent filing of a pharmaceutical product may take place immediately after the invention of the same and if found eligible, patent may be granted within 3-4 years from the date of filing. But it takes 6-10 years or even more to complete the clinical trials associated with the drug and subsequently obtain approval from regulatory agencies to launch the drug into the market. Approval from the regulatory bodies of all countries where the drug is intended to be launched is required. Henceforth, a lot of valuable time even after obtaining the patent is lost in bringing the drug from the lab to the pharmacist's shop. Regulatory agencies adhere to strict guidelines while giving approval to products made for human consumption and such approvals are based on extensive clinical trial data. In light of the above facts, it is very important to understand that out of the standard 20 years protection time in the form of patent given to an invention, fifty percent of the protection time is lost in acquiring regulatory approvals. Under such circumstances, it is important to understand that whether the remaining time left after obtaining regulatory approval is sufficient enough for the companies to earn back the money invested in research and also earn profit as well. Once the patent expires after 20 years, the invention is now available to open market and any company can manufacture and sell the same without causing any infringement. In India however, no such consideration is given for extending the patent term beyond 20 years despite understanding the fact that bulk of the patent protection time is lost in obtaining approval from regulatory agencies without which the product cannot be launched in the market. Countries like Brazil, Mexico, China, Thailand, Hong Kong etc. also have similar rule whereby patent term is non-extendable. However, countries like USA, Israel, Singapore, Russia, Taiwan, Japan, European Union etc. have provision for extending the patent term for certain products like pharmaceutical drugs, agrochemicals, food additives, medical devices etc. In the USA, patent term extension is governed by Hatch-Waxman Act, 1984. The patent term can be extended upto five years, however, the total patent term should not be more than 14 years from the date of approval of the product by US-FDA (United States Food and Drug Administration). This period may be extended by another six months with pediatric exclusivity. The European Patent Office provides an extension of protection in this regard by giving Supplementary Protection Certificate (SPC). It allows extending the patent term by 5 years, however, the total term should not be more than 15 years after the date of approval of the product by the European Medicines Agency. Additional 6 months protection is given specifically to pediatric formulations. Russia also offers an extension in the form of providing supplementary protection for 5 years for drugs, agrochemicals and pesticide.

Extension can be given either by direct extension of the patent term or by the issue of Supplementary Protection Certificate, both of them has the same objective of extending the patent protection for some limited products beyond the normal 20 years of protection. Such extension is provided by some countries to adjust the time lost in gaining regulatory approval which is a mandatory requirement for launching the product in the market (which are meant for direct or indirect human consumption)

CHAPTER 16

Patenting as a Career Option (Patent Agents)

Patent Agent is an authorized person who prosecutes patent before the Indian Patent Office. In simple language, a patent agent is a person who can be approached by the applicant for drafting, filing a patent application and also to carry out all other post filing and post grant formalities including complicated issues of patent opposition and revocation. The term authorized person mentioned above indicates that only those persons who have qualified the patent agent examination conducted by the Indian Patent Office and have registered themselves with patent office, post qualification of the examination is only authorized to practice issues related with patents before the Controller of patents. However, it may be noted that infringement cases are handled by patent attorney who are basically practicing advocates with specialization in handling patent cases. Infringement cases are prosecuted in the High Court. Whereas, a patent agent practices before the Controller of the patent office on matters related to pre-filing and post-filing issues. A patent agent may not be a law graduate but mandatorily has to be a science/engineering graduate from any recognized Indian University with more than 21 years of age. Qualifying the patent agent examination is must for registering as a patent agent and all matters related to registration of the patent agent are dealt by the Office of the Controller General of Patents, Designs and Trademarks, Mumbai. The exam for patent agent is generally conducted annually whose notification is provided on the Indian patent website. The exam forms can be filled online (http://ipindiaonline.gov.in/AgentExam2020/User/frmLogin.aspx) and the payment for the same can be made online as well. In the current innovation driven world, career as a patent agent has become a lucrative option these days for any science graduate. The COVID-19 pandemic has taught and also made us to practice the art of work from home. Patent agent job is a perfect example of 'job from home'. The biggest strength of companies are their innovations which leads to products for human use. Such innovations have to be protected by acquiring IP rights and proper vigilance is also required on any possible threats arising due to infringements. As a result, many companies hire full time and part time patent attorneys and patent agents for taking care and preserving their IP assets. Patent attorneys basically looks after infringement cases in the High Court whereas, paten agents' primary job is to get the paper work done for acquiring the IPR and to discharge duties associated with patent proceedings before the Controller (Section 127 of Indian Patents Act). Patent agents also play a vital role in patent search and preparing technology landscape which are vital tools for innovation in the modern era. Patent agent is also an interesting career for women candidates who have got a break in their career due to fulfillment of social/personal commitments and wants to return to main stream. Such persons can prepare for the patent agent exams and start practicing as a free lancer or may work for a law firm. Since such work needs intellect and computer facilities only, henceforth work can be easily done form the comfort of one's own home. The format of question paper for patent agent examination is given below,

TABLE 16.1 Question paper format for patent agent examination.

Paper	Marks allotted	Pattern of question
Paper I = 100 marks (time allotted is 2 hours & no negative marking) More than one correct option may be possible and if so, the same shall be indicated in the question paper Topic: Patent Rules		
Part A	60	MCQ (30 questions×2)
Part B	10	True/False combination (10 questions×1)
Part C	30	MCQ (10 questions×3)
Paper II = 100 marks (time allotted is 3 hours & no negative marking) All questions are descriptive type Topic: Patent Rules		
Part A	20	Descriptive questions (4 questions×5)
Part B	30	Descriptive questions and case studies (3 questions×10)
Part C1	20	Details of an invention shall be provided. Title of the invention, claims and abstract have to be constructed (out of two questions, one has to be attempted)

Table 16.1 *Contd....*

<table>
<tr><th>Paper</th><th>Marks allotted</th><th>Pattern of question</th></tr>
<tr><td>Part C2</td><td>30</td><td>Details of an invention shall be provided. Complete specification shall be asked to be drafted including claims (out of two questions, one has to be attempted)</td></tr>
<tr><td>Viva-voce</td><td>100</td><td>Based on domain knowledge only</td></tr>
<tr><td colspan="3">• The passing score is minimum 50% in each paper and the minimum overall aggregate required is 60%
• There are no fixed number of seats
• Examination is conducted in various centres throughout India
• There is no upper age limit
• There are no restrictions on the number of attempts
• Patent agent job is not exclusively for lawyers, any science graduate above 21 years of age can appear for the exam
• Patent agent can practice while already in a job
• No specific job location, can work from home also</td></tr>
</table>

The difference between a patent agent and patent attorney is given below for easy understanding of the readers,

Patent agent	Patent attorney
Minim degree required: Science graduate	Minim degree required: Law + Science degree
Deals with pre-filing and post-filing matters	Deals with infringement cases
Can draft and file a patent application	Cannot file a patent application unless qualifies the patent agent examination
Practices before the Indian patent office	Practices before the court of law
Must be registered with the Indian patent office	Must be registered with the Bar Council of India

Patent agents are governed by section 125-127 of the Indian Patents Act. After qualifying the patent agent exam, the candidate has to register oneself with the Indian patent office by applying in Form-22. The register of patent agents shall contain vital information regarding the name, citizenship, address, qualification, specimen signatures, photograph, date of registration and renewal status of every registered patent agent. Such register is maintained digitally and can be accessed only by the Controller or any officer authorized by the Controller.

<table>
<tr><td colspan="2" align="center">Sample copy
FORM 22
THE PATENTS ACT, 1970
(39 OF 1970)
AND
THE PATENTS RULES, 2003
APPLICATION FOR REGISTRATION OF PATENT AGENT
(See rules 109(1) and 112)</td></tr>
<tr><td>1. Certificate testifying to the character of the applicant should be from a person not related to him and being a Gazetted Officer or any other person whom the Controller thinks fit</td><td>I beg to apply for registration as a patent agent under the Patents Act, 1970.
A certificate of character from ……… is enclosed herewith.
I hereby declare than I am not subject to any of the disqualifications specified in rule 114 of the Patent Rules, 2003 and that the information given below is true to the best of my knowledge and belief.</td></tr>
<tr><td>2. Family or principal name in the beginning.</td><td>1. Name …….
2. Address/place of residence ………
3. Principal place of business …………..
4. Address of the branch office if any ……
5. Father's name: ……
6. Nationality: …….
7. Date and place of birth …………
8. Occupation ………..</td></tr>
<tr><td>3. Either original certificates and other documents or copies thereof duly attested by the Gazetted Officer or any other person whom the Controller thinks fit must be sent with the application</td><td>9. Particulars of qualification for registration as patent agent.
a. …….
b. ……
c. …….</td></tr>
<tr><td>4. To be signed by the applicant</td><td>Dated this ……. Day of …… 20….
Signature ………………….</td></tr>
<tr><td>5. Name of the natural person who has signed</td><td>…………………………..</td></tr>
<tr><td></td><td>To
The Controller ofPatents
The Patent Office
At ………</td></tr>
</table>

A registered patent agent shall be disqualified as a patent agent if,

- Insane
- Bankrupt
- If, bankrupted, has not obtained an order from the court that such act was a result of misfortune and not of any misconduct
- Convicted by a court of law (including any conviction faced outside India) leading to imprisonment, unless pardoned
- Found guilty of professional misconduct including financial misconduct (also if being a chartered account).

In case of a law firm to be registered as a patent agent, all the legal partners of the firm should register themselves as patent agent first. The Controller of Patents only or any authorized person by him should have access to the register of patent agents. Once entered, the name of the patent agent can be removed from the official register as per Section 130 of Indian Patents Act, if he is found to disqualify on the grounds mentioned, if name was entered by mistake or misrepresented, not paid his renewal fees, requested by the person himself, death of patent agent or if the patent agent is no more a citizen of India. Restoration of any removed name is possible on application in Form-23 within two months from such removal, the same shall also be published on the patent office website and communicated to the respective person. Even any alteration of name, address or contact details if requested by the patent agent shall also be published upon approval.

CHAPTER 17

Patent Search

Patent search refers to searching of granted patents or published patent applications which are being processed. Depending upon the purpose of the search, patent search can be divided into the following types,

(a) *Prior art search*: this is basically done using some key words and is a broad search to find out the patentability of the invention. In simpler words, before seeking protection for an invention, it is desirable to carry out a patentability search by checking the number of prior arts that are available in terms of patent literature by conducting a search through some patent databases. It may be noted that search for non-patent literature is also required for determining the patentability aspect but in this topic only patent literature shall be discussed. The claims of the invention which are being revealed from the search through patent databases, should be studied to check the patentability scope. The basic objective of such search is to determine the novelty and inventive step of the invention so that the applicant or his attorney can understand the chances of patent being granted, if filed.

(b) *Validity/invalidity search*: such type of search is conducted after issuance of patent, mostly by competitors who may make an attempt to invalidate a granted patent which is likely to affect their business by producing relevant prior art which is likely to destroy the novelty or inventive step of the invention which has been granted patent. When such search is carried out to invalidate a patent, it is known as invalidity search. On the other hand, the patentee shall also carry out search to prove the validity of his patent, in such case it becomes validity search.

(c) *Freedom to operate search (FTO)*: such search for patent literature from patent databases in very important when a company is planning to bring out a particular product in the market. At such a point, it is very important to see whether somebody's patent is getting infringed by the said product or not. Any kind of resulting infringements can bring about heavy financial loss for the infringing company apart from other legal complications. Such search is not limited to key words but is rather a very close and narrow search. Using specific keywords could be risky because a same product can be described in different ways and searching through specific keywords may not provide conclusive search results required to abolish any fear of infringements. Such kind of search of patent literature are performed on specific competitors who deals with similar product line. Search can be specific to some country only where the product is intended to launch. A product if patented in India, is valid in India only and the same product if not patented in other foreign country then it can be used freely by others in foreign countries without the consent of the patentee and without causing any infringement issues. Search in case of determining FTO can also be limited to 20 years search period or to any technical field depending upon the international patent classification.

(d) *Landscape search*: carried out by companies engaged in R&D and researchers to understand the technological evolutions in a particular scientific field through prior art documents. It helps in planning better research activities by identifying the gaps in research by studying the prior art documents. Appropriate IP strategy can also be planned based on landscape search.

Some of the patent databases which are available for patent searching are

1. Indian patent office (free)
2. Google patents (free) – does not include Australian patents
3. LexisNexis TotalPatent One (https://www.lexisnexisip.com/products/totalpatent-one/) – subscription based
4. LENS.ORG (https://www.lens.org/) – free and includes Australian patents also
5. Espacenet (https://worldwide.espacenet.com/) – free
6. AusPat (http://pericles.ipaustralia.gov.au/ols/auspat/quickSearch.do) – for Australian patents
7. PATENTSCOPE (https://patentscope.wipo.int/search/en/search.jsf) – provides free access to published PCT applications
8. THOMSON INNOVATION (https://clarivate.com/derwent/solutions/derwent-innovation/) – subscription based

CHAPTER 18

Treaties and Conventions

18.1 Summary

World Intellectual Property Organization (WIPO) is headquartered at Geneva, Switzerland and is a committed organization for protection of intellectual property at the global platform. World Intellectual Property Organization came into existence through the WIPO convention signed on July 14, 1967 in Stockholm, which entered into force in 1970 and amended in 1979. In 1974 WIPO became a specialized agency of United Nations. The foundation for the birth of WIPO was laid by two major events, the Paris Convention for the Protection of Industrial Property and the Berne Convention for the Protection of Literary and Artistic Works in 1883 and 1886, respectively. In the both the conventions, a deep need for the existence of an 'International Bureau' was heavily felt by the participating member countries. The two organizations, which had established separate secretariats to enforce their respective treaties, merged in 1893 to become the United International Bureau for the Protection of Intellectual Property (BIRPI), which was based in Bern, Switzerland and was considered as WIPO's immediate predecessor. Finally BIRPI gets transformed into a member state-led intergovernmental organization named WIPO, with its headquarters based in Geneva, Switzerland.

The two basic objectives of WIPO are (a) promotion of protection of intellectual property at the global platform and (b) to extent administrative support among the intellectual property Unions established by the various treaties administered by WIPO.

Functions of WIPO:

- Improvement of IP protection at the global level and to develop a uniform legislation in this regard
- Signing and implementation of international agreements on IP protection including establishing appropriate standards for the enforcement of IP rights
- Administrative support to the Unions of Paris and Berne signatory members

- Technical and legal support in the field of intellectual property rights
- Rendering services regarding filing of international applications for protection of intellectual properties
- Research and publication.

Currently WIPO, is committed to use IP assets for negotiating diseases like neglected tropical diseases, tuberculosis/ malaria which has badly affected the mankind and gender equality where WIPO is committed to empowering women through IP knowledge. The secretariat office of the WIPO is known as the International Bureau. The executive head of WIPO is known as the Director General appointed by the WIPO General Assembly, who is further subordinated by two or more Deputy Directors General. Currently a Singapore national Daren Tang, is the Director General of WIPO who has started office since October 1st, 2020. Currently there are 193 member states of WIPO. India, became a member of WIPO in 1975 and is currently signatory to six treaties administered by WIPO, such as WIPO Convention (1975), Paris Convention (1998), Berne Convention (1928), Patent Cooperation Treaty (1998), Phonograms Convention (1975) and Nairobi Treaty on the Protection of Olympic Symbol.

Treaties administered by WIPO

Treaties administered by WIPO		
Treaty	**Year**	**Description**
Treaties on Industrial Property		
Paris Convention for the Protection of Industrial Property	(1883)	Provides to twelve months additional time after filing basic application in home country (has to be a member of Paris Convention) for filing in other member states with full protection of priority date.
Madrid Agreement Concerning the International Registration of Marks and the Protocol Relating to that Agreement	1891 and 1989	Allows international registration for protection of marks that has the same effect in all contracting states. May be filed only by a natural person or legal entity possessing a link with the contracting state in terms of establishment, domicile or nationality. The date of effect of registration in each of the contracting state is the date of filing the international registration and each member state shall consider as if the application has been filed directly in their regional office. Separate filing of application for registration of marks in different countries and in respective languages is not required, filing of a single international application is enough. The tenure of international registration is for 10 years subjected to further renewal on payment of prescribed fees.

Contd...

Treaties administered by WIPO		
Treaty	**Year**	**Description**
Madrid Agreement for the Repression of False or Deceptive Indications of Source on Goods (1891)	1891	Import of any such goods having a false or misleading information on source of origin whereby one of the contracting states is indicated falsely as a source of origin of such goods resulting in deceiving the public, must be banned or seized upon importation. The act allows provision of such seizure.
Hague Agreement Concerning the International Registration of Industrial Designs (1925)	1925	Two Acts of the Hague Agreement are currently in operation, the 1999 Act and the 1960 Act. Through the provisions laid down by this act, applicants can register their industrial designs in multiple member countries by filing a single international application with the International Bureau of WIPO with minimum paperwork involved. Renewal is also possible through a single international application.
Nice Agreement Concerning the International Classification of Goods and Services for the Purposes of the Registration of Marks (1957)	1957	The Nice Agreement dictates classification of goods and services for the purposes of registering trademarks and service marks (the Nice Classification). The Agreement, concluded in 1957, was revised at Stockholm in 1967 and at Geneva in 1977, and was amended in 1979.
Lisbon Agreement for the Protection of Appellations of Origin and their International Registration	1958	The Lisbon Agreement provides provision for the protection of appellations of origin, which is a special kind of geographical indication consisting of a traditional designation given on the product which have a special quality or typical characteristics which is exclusively due to the geographical environment (including nature and human) in which they are produced. Such denominations are registered by the International Bureau of WIPO in Geneva upon the request of the competent authority of a Contracting State.
Locarno Agreement Establishing an International Classification for Industrial Designs (1968)	1968	The Locarno Agreement establishes a classification system for industrial designs known as the Locarno Classification. The competent offices of the member countries must mention in their official documents the registration of industrial designs and the numbers of the classes and subclasses of the classification to which the goods incorporating the designs belong. The classification system contains 32 classes and 219 subclasses along with an alphabetical list of goods with an indication of the class and subclass to which each product belongs.

Contd...

Treaties administered by WIPO		
Treaty	**Year**	**Description**
Patent Cooperation Treaty (PCT) (1970)	1970	Allows inventors to seek patent protection in large number of member countries by filing a single international application with preservation of priority date, provided such international application is filed within 12 months from basic filing. Ensures national treatment for all foreign applicants
Strasbourg Agreement Concerning the International Patent Classification (1971)	1971	Establishes the International Patent Classification (IPC) system dividing all sorts of technological inventions into eight sections with approximately 70,000 subdivisions. Each subdivision is further indicated by a combination of Arabic numerals and Latin alphabets. The appropriate symbols are allotted by the national or regional patent office that publishes the patent document. For PCT applications, IPC symbols are allotted by the International Searching Authority. Such classification helps in retrieving patent literature during prior art search.
Vienna Agreement Establishing an International Classification of the Figurative Elements of Marks (1973)	1973	Establishes the Vienna Classification for marks that consist of, or contain, figurative elements. The competent offices of member countries must indicate the same in their official documents and publications relating to registrations and renewals of marks and the numbers of the categories, divisions and sections of the Classification to which the figurative elements of those marks belong.
Budapest Treaty on the International Recognition of the Deposit of Microorganisms for the Purposes of Patent Procedure (1977)	1977	All member states agree to deposit microorganism sample for the purpose of patenting, in any designated International Depository Authority (ISA) and provide the accession number during filing of the patent application. Such sample shall be open for public inspection after publication of the patent application
Nairobi Treaty on the Protection of the Olympic Symbol (1981)	1981	All countries signatory to the Nairobi Treaty must protect the Olympic symbol which is five interlaced rings against any commercial purpose in their respective country (like advertisement in any goods for increasing its sell). If the International Olympic Committee grants any authorization for the use of the Olympic symbol to any member country, then the National Olympic Committee of that State is entitled to a part of the revenue, which the International Olympic Committee may earn from such permission deal.

Contd...

Treaties administered by WIPO		
Treaty	**Year**	**Description**
Trademark Law Treaty (TLT) (1994)	1994	Main aim of this treaty was to standardize and streamline national and international trademark registration process by developing a uniform simple process for member countries so that trademark registration in multiple countries becomes simple and more predictable. Three main phases have been described with simple explanatory rules in the process of trademark registration namely, application-changes after registration -renewal.
Patent Law Treaty (PLT) (2000)	2000	Provides minimum requirements for obtaining a filing date after submission of patent application, standardization of the requirements of patent application, simplification of patent office procedures and facilitation of e-filing while ensuring that paper filing stays.
Singapore Treaty on the Law of Trademarks (2006)	2006	The main objective of this treaty is to create a dynamic framework for the harmonization of administrative trademark registration procedures.
Treaties related to Copyright and associated rights		
Berne Convention for the Protection of Literary and Artistic Works (1886)	1886	Protects the of work and the rights of their authors. The treaty provides minimum protection to be granted and specifies certain special provisions to be given to developing countries regarding use of such protected works. It has three basic principles namely, the work which originated in one member country shall be given the same protection status in all member countries just the same way each member country would have protected the work of their own citizens (national treatment), principle of automatic protection should be implemented and no conditions should be imposed and protection in member countries shall be independent of the existence of protection in the originating country.
Rome Convention for the Protection of Performers, Producers of Phonograms and Broadcasting Organisations (1961)	1961	The Rome Convention provides protection in performances for performers (actors, singers, musicians, dancers and those who perform literary or artistic works), in phonograms for producers of phonograms and in broadcasts for broadcasting organizations.

Contd...

Treaties administered by WIPO		
Treaty	**Year**	**Description**
Geneva Convention for the Protection of Producers of Phonograms Against Unauthorized Duplication of their Phonograms (1971)	1971	Phonogram is an aural fixation. The convention obligates all member countries to protect a producer of a phonogram who is a citizen of another member country against any unauthorized making of duplicates in the member countries or importation of such duplicates in the country for the purpose of distribution to public. Protection must be provided for at least 20 years from the date of first publication of the phonogram.
Brussels Convention Relating to the Distribution of Programme-Carrying Signals Transmitted by Satellite (1974)	1974	The Brussels Convention makes it obligatory for each member countries to take necessary preventive measures for prevention of unauthorized distribution (not authorized by the broadcasting organization) on or from its territory of any programme-carrying signal transmitted by satellite. The obligation exists in respect of organizations that are nationals of a member State.
WIPO Copyright Treaty (WCT) (1996)	1996	Special agreement under the Berne Convention that deals with the protection of works and the rights of their authors in the digital environment. The term of protection must be at least 50 years for any kind of work.
WIPO Performances and Phonograms Treaty (WPPT) (1996)	1996	Deals with the rights of two kinds of beneficiaries, especially in the digital environment: (a) performers (actors, singers, musicians, etc.); and (b) producers of phonograms. Performers are granted economic rights in their performances fixed in phonograms such as right of reproduction, right of distribution, right of rental and right of making available along with moral rights.
Beijing Treaty on Audio-visual Performances (2012)	2012	The Treaty deals with the IPR of performers with regard to audio-visual performances. It grants performers four kinds of economic rights for their performances fixed namely, the right of reproduction, the right of distribution, the right of rental and the right of making available.
Marrakesh Treaty to Facilitate Access to Published Works for Persons who Are Blind, Visually Impaired, or Otherwise Print Disabled (MVT) (2013)	2013	Its main objective is to establish a set of mandatory limitations and exceptions for the benefit of the blind, visually impaired and otherwise print disabled (VIPs). It makes member countries to frame standard set of limitations and exceptions to copyright rules in order to permit reproduction, distribution and making available of published works in formats designed to be accessible to VIPs, and to permit exchange of these works across borders by organizations that serve those beneficiaries.

18.2 Paris Convention – 1883

The Paris Convention born in 1883 was enacted for the protection of a broad spectrum of industrial properties such as patents, trademarks, industrial designs, utility models, trade names and geographical indications. This international treaty was the first global effort for protection of various intellectual properties of different creators at global level. The need for this type of international common consent or agreement was felt when different international exhibitors refused to present their inventions at the International Exhibition of Inventions in Vienna and Austria in 1873. This refusal was out of the fear that the innovations if presented could have been stolen and commercially exploited in different countries by other exhibitors. Henceforth, a need was felt, to provide a sense of assurance of protection to different global creators with respect to protection of their intellectual property in regard to the fact that their intellectual creation shall be protected in other countries (by giving the same national status), in the same manner as that particular country would have protected the invention, if filed by their own nationals. Initially only 11 countries namely, Belgium, Brazil, France, Guatemala, Italy, The Netherlands, Portugal, El Salvador, Serbia, Spain and Switzerland were the members of the Paris Convention when it came into existence in 1883. India became a member of the Paris Convention in 1998. Paris convention can be understood in light of the three major rights which it accords upon its member countries.

(i) *National Treatment*: every member country of Paris Convention is bound to provide the same national treatment to all foreign applications coming from other member countries who are signatory to Paris Convention. Such foreign applications shall be given the same importance and treatment what otherwise would have been given to an application filed by their own nationals.

(ii) *Right of priority*: it indicates that if a patents, marks and industrial designs have been filed as a first basic application in any of the member countries, followed by subsequent filing of the same application in other member countries with twelve months of filing the basic application (six months for industrial designs and marks), priority date shall be preserved in all member countries where subsequent filing has taken place. All member countries in such circumstances are bound to give the same priority date to the application as applicable for the first basic filing.

Example: application filed in India (basic application) – 1st January 2020, same invention filed in France (member country) – 1st October 2020, same invention filed in Spain (another member country) – 1st November, 2020.

Since France and Spain are all member countries, hence they shall accord the same status to the concerned Indian application as they would have given to an application filed by their own nationals. Also, according to the treaty, since the application in France and Spain was filed within twelve months from the filing of basic application, hence the priority date of 1st January 2020 shall be preserved and the application filed in France and Spain shall have the same priority date as that of the basic application which in this case is 1st January 2020. Henceforth, any publication or usage of similar invention if taken place between 2nd January, 2020 (after filing of basic application) and before filing in any member country shall not destroy the novelty of the application and the filed invention will be given priority over those inventions occurring in the passage of time between filing the basic application and filing in any convention country within prescribed twelve months' time. Applicants gets a time window of twelve months after filing a basic application in any convention country (preferably to start with their home country, assuming the same to be a convention country as well) to decide and arrange for revenue for filing in other convention countries for seeking protection of their invention globally.

(iii) *Common rules.* Patent rules are regulated domestically which means every country has their own rules of patenting. What may be patentable in one country may be non-patentable in another country. Hence all member countries will treat the application as per their domestic rules. If an application has been rejected in any member country, the same cannot form basis for rejection in other member country. Every member country shall treat the application individually, irrespective of whether the application is being accepted or rejected in other member countries. A patent application may not be rejected or a granted patent may not be invalidated in any member country on the grounds that the product arising out of the invention couldn't be commercialized in the applicants' home country, subjected to restrictions resulting from domestic law. Also, sufficient sensitivity should be maintained regarding grant of compulsory license to any invention by any member country, in this regard the patentee must also be heard on why the patent could not be commercialized because of which grant of compulsory license is being considered. The same perception also exists for registration of marks. If a mark applied for registration gets denied in a home country due to prevailing domestic law, such results may not have any implication on the registration of the said mark in other member countries. Each member country where the applicant has filed for registration of mark shall treat the matter individually according to their domestic laws without being influence by the decision of other member countries.

18.3 PCT

Patent Cooperation Treaty, 1970 enables a person to file an international patent application for seeking protection in a large number of countries who are members of PCT. Patent is a territorial right and often the inventor needs to seek protection in multiple foreign countries where his invention is likely to be used. In this regard PCT provides an excellent opportunity for filing in multiple countries with a single international application along with preservation of priority date. According to the treaty, the applicant can start preferably by filing a patent application in his home country which is considered as the basic application. The filing date of the basic application becomes the priority date. As per PCT, the applicant gets a 12 months window to file an international application with any Receiving Office or WIPO and for this time period the priority date is preserved. This means that if an applicant files an international application say after nine months, he is eligible to get the same priority date as applicable for the basic application. During filing of the international application, the applicant designates those member countries where he desires the application to enter. The PCT is just a route for seeking protection in designated member countries with protection of priority date. The PCT route has some processing which also includes an international search report along with a written opinion intending to help the applicant to understand the patentability strength of his application and the applicant also gets an opportunity to make amendments in light of the facts revealed from the search report. After the expiry of 30/31 months from the priority date, the international application enters the designated member countries where the application is examined as per the domestic patent laws of that particular country. The details of PCT processing are explained in 'Foreign Filing' chapter.

18.4 TRIPS Agreement along with DOHA Declaration

Intellectual property which is the creativity of human mind either in the form of an invention, design, trademark, literary, artistic works etc. are actually the assets of any country. Directly or indirectly such human creations greatly affect the trade related aspects of every country and international trade as well. The involvement and contributions of such intellectual creations of human mind in international trade is enormous and if adequate protection to such intellectual property is not provided, trade aspects may get dismantled. Even though, such protection of intellectual properties do exist in many developed countries but still there were many countries where such framework was either not available or even if available was too inadequate to offer all round stable protection to such creations. In light of the above-mentioned fact, a strong inconsistency was observed between countries with matters related to providing protection to intellectual properties to enhance trade, thus a need to establish minimum uniform standards among the agreed countries was deeply felt. Already there were in place some treaties such as Paris Convention and Berne convention for protection of intellectual creations but there was a need for a common treaty for creating uniform trade related aspects of intellectual property, largely to boost global trade. However, with more emphasis being placed on the trade-related aspects of intellectual property, an urgent need was felt to establish an international agreement in the context of GATT, with maximum nations participating to establish common international standards of protection of intellectual property associated with trade. In light of the above fact, Trade-Related Aspects of Intellectual Property Rights (TRIPS) became one of the focused areas for discussion at the Uruguay Round of GATT, which began in 1986. Along with other agreements to come out of the Uruguay Round, the Agreement on Trade-Related Aspects of Intellectual Property Rights (the TRIPS Agreement), a multilateral intellectual property agreement was finally agreed upon at the ministerial meeting in Marrakesh, Morocco in April 1994, and came into force as part of the WTO Agreement on January 1st, 1995. The four key issues of TRIPS which were consented upon were,

- Uniform international standard norms of IPR protection
- Creating national laws by respective countries for enforcement of IPR protection
- Settlement of dispute between parties
- Interrelationship of TRIPS with other agreements like GATT and organizations like WIPO and treaties administered by WIPO.

The TRIPS agreement is a very comprehensive treaty with 73 articles divided into seven parts. The first part sets the general provisions and basic principles which clearly indicates that member countries have to develop and enact their own domestic laws to implement all the features of TRIPS agreement which defines all types of 'intellectual property' like patents, copyright, designs etc. Further, the TRIPS Agreement provides that Members shall comply and oblige with other existing treaties associated with intellectual property rights like the Paris Convention and Berne Convention. These treaties accord national treatment which means that applications coming from other member countries for protection of intellectual properties shall be accorded the same national status as the receiving member country would have given to the nationals of their country. The TRIPS Agreement's (article 4) made way for another treatment called the most-favoured-nation treatment with regard to the protection of intellectual property. It indicates that any advantage, favour, privilege or immunity granted by a member to the nationals of any other country shall be accorded immediately and unconditionally to the nationals of all other members as well. In simpler words, countries cannot discriminate between their trading partners and granting someone special privilege shall mean granting the same privilege to all member countries. Part II of the TRIPS Agreement provides minimum standards, scope and use of intellectual property rights such as patents, copyrights, trademarks etc. Part III of the agreement contains detailed provisions regarding general obligations, civil and administrative procedures and remedies available, provisional measures, special requirements related to border measures, and criminal procedures (members shall make provision for criminal procedures and penalties in cases related trademark counterfeiting or copyright piracy on a commercial scale. Remedies may include imprisonment and/or monetary fines sufficient to provide a deterrent). Part IV mentions acquisition and maintenance standards of IPR, Part V refers to dispute prevention and settlement arising out of the implementation of TRIPS agreement including maintenance of transparency with one's internal laws, Part VI reflects provisional arrangements indicating transitional arrangements for the implementation of TRIPS by lesser developed countries and Part VII dictates institutional arrangements and final provisions which states that Council for TRIPS shall monitor the operation of this Agreement and compliance of member countries and shall afford members the opportunity of consulting on matters relating to the trade-related aspects of intellectual property rights. Members also agreed to refrain from practising such trades of goods which involves infringing intellectual property rights.

A special ministerial declaration at the WTO Ministerial Conference in DOHA (known as the DOHA Declaration on the TRIPS Agreement and Public Health) in 2001 was adopted related to taking measures by the member countries to protect public health. There was a growing concern regarding availability of patented drugs which are required to control diseases of public health like HIV, tuberculosis, malaria etc. in developing countries or poor countries. The said declaration agreed upon at DOHA was basically on providing such patented drugs at an affordable price to developing/under developed countries in the larger interest of public health. Thus, protection of public health and enhanced access to patented drugs at affordable prices during public health crisis to poor countries was the major agenda of the DOHA declaration. The above agenda can be implemented through compulsory licences which empowers the government to licence the production of the patented drug to a third party without the consent of the patentee. When such licenses are granted during situations of health crisis, certain requirements are waived to speed up the process of production of such drugs. The DOHA Declarations states that each member country has the right to grant such licences and flexibility and also to determine the grounds upon which such licences are granted. DOHA Declaration also made way for parallel importation of patented products without the consent of the patent holder where the said products are marketed in another country. Since many drugs are sold at different prices in different countries, through parallel importation, government can import lower priced patented drugs so that access to life saving drugs can be provided to the public at large. The DOHA Declaration also provided 10 years extension in transition period for least developed countries for the implementation of the TRIPS obligations.

CHAPTER 19

National IPR Policy

Creativity and innovation fuel the development of any knowledge economy. An abundance of innovation exists in India which needs to be channelized in a committed direction. Lack of awareness towards seeking protection for intellectual properties has been one of the retarding factors for India's innovation strength. India has a sound intellectual property legislation and associated jurisprudence framework to provide a conducive ecosystem for the Indian innovators to exercise their innovation to the fullest strength in a secured intellectual property right framework. This led to an evolvement of the National IPR Policy primarily intended to nurture the culture of innovation to its fullest potential and at the same time have a strong framework to protect such rights and utilize then to India's wealth creation through an efficient administrative procedural mechanism. The national IPR Policy was approved on the 12thMay, 2016 by the Union Government which is expected to lay a roadmap for IPR's in India with a clarity to make India an innovation rich nation.

The policy encompasses seven golden principles which are to be implemented by the concerned Ministry for attaining the objectives behind the policy.

1. *Outreach & Promotion*: Aims in propagating the values of transforming knowledge into innovation with a clarity on protecting the same through acquiring IP rights. The policy makers have taken a clear note of the fact that the chain of disinterest shown towards IP protection by Indian innovators needs to be broken. Indian innovators often exhibit such disinterest due to lack of knowledge towards acquiring IP protection or inability to understand the financial and economic strength of such IPR. Henceforth, the policy makers have emphasized upon a nation-wide campaign to improve the awareness level of Indian innovators towards IPR. Through various outreach programmes a conducive environment for all types of innovators may be provided where they can exercise creativity and innovation with a fearless mind. Such outreach programmes shall target less visible

innovators who are not frontline innovators, situated in rural areas. Innovation shall lead to a sense of pride and help in character building, leading to nation building in a holistic way. The following steps were suggested by the policy makers in order to achieve the intended target,

- Infusion of the slogan 'Creative India: Innovative India' into the society through various channels and integration of the campaign with other various ongoing government initiatives
- Promoting values and benefits of IP by targeting silent and less aware innovators in rural areas to increase their understanding on the subject, creating IP ambassadors by involving famous and eminent personalities who can inspire other or may act as role models for others and using audio/visual/print/electronic media for awareness propagation, sharing of success stories and highlighting case studies of successful countries
- Publicizing various events to project the significance of IP through various partnership programmes with corporates, celebrating IP dedicated days, creating 'Hall of Fame' to honour Indian innovators etc.
- Preparing desired course material to ensure IP awareness through inclusion of such course materials in curriculum at both school and University level either by classroom learning or through other online platforms

2. *Generation of IPR's*: Emphasizes on increasing IP filings. India has an appreciable filing rate for trademarks, copyrights, geographical indications but the filing needs to improve for patents and designs. An elaborate IP audit in all sectors shall be carried out to identify all possible existing potentials and subsequently develop customized committed programmes to utilize such potentials to seek new IPR's in all sectors. Some of the significant steps suggested by the policy makers in order to generate greater amount of IPR's are as follows,
    - Integrate use of various ongoing government initiatives to develop a culture of innovation and IPR
    - IP audit to identify various areas of strengths and potential and prioritize target groups and try to address their needs in acquiring IPR's
    - Devising strategies to improve IPR outcomes of various educational and research institutions
    - Encouraging research and provide necessary guidance to researchers to focus on national priority areas
    - Establish IP facilitation centers and nodal points

- Consider providing suitable incentives for innovators
- Simple loan guarantee scheme to encourage start-ups
- Radius of TKDL to be expanded and its access reach to be increased for further research
- Awareness on international filing machineries
- IPR generation for ICT technologies

3. *Legal & Legislative Frameworks*: Innovation is important for boost of economy but it is equally important to provide a strong and balanced legal ecosystem for the protection of such innovations. Optimized legislation related to IPR which is consistent and in compliance with various international agreements (like TRIPS), is necessary in making fullest use of all sorts of inventions and encouraging all inventors to practice such types of inventions beneficial for mankind. Policy makers have taken a due note of the above facts and have understood that in a dynamic knowledge society, it is very important that legislations related to IPR should also be updated to ensure a safe environment for innovators to operate and also for making legislations in resonance with national priorities. Policy makers have also emphasized the need of a strong IPR legislation for protecting India's rich traditional knowledge and at the same time providing enough secured space for utilizing such knowledge for the benefit of mankind. On one hand where the policy talks about strengthening the legal framework, but at the same time also emphasizes on providing sufficient transparency while administering the different provisions mentioned in various acts related to IPR. The steps suggested by the policy makers to attain the above-mentioned objectives are,
   - Continuous upgradation of IPR legislation to bring about clarity and remove any ambiguity in the law
   - To ensure that the existing IP laws are in resonance with the standards prescribed in various international laws and treaties
   - To be member of all such international treaties which will further empower our own legal framework and provide an IP secured environment for national and international innovators
   - Continually engage in various constructive negotiations and deliberations at various international platform and make binding laws for the protection of our traditional knowledge and genetic resources
   - IP laws should facilitate technology transfer and adoption of clean technologies and show their sensitiveness towards climate change

4. *Administration & Management*: Intellectual Property Offices (IPO's) are constantly engaged in rendering different IP oriented services to the users at the quickest possible manner. The policy makers have noted that with time there have been rapid increase in applications seeking IPR protection and also in the complications arising out of the processing of such applications as well. Henceforth, the IPOs should develop their ICT enabled infrastructure and operative procedures to enable themselves to handle the ever-increasing load of IPRs both at the national and international level. The IPO of India should be at par with other international offices in terms of ICT infrastructure and management. In this regard, sensitizing of IPR officials and capacity building is necessary where RGNIIPM can play a pivotal role. In order to promote generation and commercialization of IP assets, a cell for IPR Promotions and Management (CIPAM) needs to be created under the DPIIT. Necessity of continuous symbiotic link between India's patent offices and those with other countries was also realized by the policy makers. Some of the important steps that were suggested by the policy makers to achieve the above-mentioned goals towards modernization and empowering IPR administration are as follows,

    - Transfer of power for administering Copyright act, 1957 from Department of Higher Education to Department for Promotion of Industry and Internal Trade (DPIIT)
    - Transfer of power for administering Integrated Circuits Layout Design Act, 2000 from Department of Electronic and Information Technology to DPIIT
    - Infrastructural upgradation of IPOs along with manpower recruitment and re-configuration of cadres
    - Collaboration of IPO's with educational institutions and others
    - Implementation of TKDL as minimum requirement in PCT documentation
    - Capacity building in collaboration with IPOs of other countries
    - Adoption of best office practices for rendering smooth IP services along with the creation of a service-oriented work culture

- Significant changes in the structure of Copyright, Protection of Plant Varieties and Semiconductors Integrated Circuits Layout Design rules for increasing its inclusiveness
- Integration of National Biodiversity Authority with IPOs and other concerned ministries or department's

5. *Commercialization of IPR's*: A true reward for an invention is its commercialization which is the only way to use the innovations to their fullest potential in strengthening the economy of the country. Entrepreneurship plays a critical role in this regard. Policy makers have cited that different government agencies like BIRAC, TIFAC should proactively handle any financial crunch situation that might resist entrepreneurs in commercializing their innovations. IP facilitation centers synchronized with industry must be set up for providing ease for commercialization. Some of the significant suggestions provided by the policy makers are,
    - CIPAM to play leadership role in creating a common platform and database for innovators and potential users or buyers of IP
    - Set up best practices in IP commercialization through smooth licensing guidelines for providing ease for commercialization and faster regulatory processes to ensure timely manufacturing of drugs and chemicals
    - Financial support to less empowered IP owners like farmers, artisans, craftsmen etc. by offering friendly loans
    - Promoting going-to-market activities through validation of pilot studies, seed funding for marketing activities, e-commerce assistance and encouragement for creating brand equity from IP rights.
6. *Enforcement and Adjudication*: Once the IP rights are obtained, it is equally important to protect the same against encroachment and the onus to do so lies on the IP owner. The IP legislation of India provides several legal remedies to the IP owners for the enforcement of their IP rights. At the same time, it is equally important to understand and balance the rights of the public as well to provide an amicable environment for all round economic development and also preventing misuse of IP rights by the owners. Policy makers have very well understood and acknowledged the need to sensitize the innovators towards protecting and enforcement of their IP rights and also at the same time there should be enough capacity building of the legal agencies responsible for enforcing such rights. Counterfeiting and piracy to be strictly dealt with and should be in compliance

with the preventive measures as suggested in TRIPS agreement. Specialized commercial courts and other alternative dispute mechanism should also be thought of and explored to adjudicate on IPR disputes. Some of the major steps suggested by the policy makers in this regard are,

- Creating IP awareness and developing an IP respect culture by connecting to all sectors of industries, educating general public and sensitizing inventors
- Strong measures to prevent counterfeiting, privacy and misappropriation of traditional knowledge in other countries
- Assistance to lesser capable bodies regarding protection of their IPR in foreign countries
- Empowering the enforcement mechanism
- Adoption of good licensing practices

7. *Human Capital Development*: This particular objective talks about developing a national capacity for providing thought leadership in the field of IPR. Considering the dynamics of the IP world, which has a rapidly changing configuration, it is very important to develop an evergreen pool of IP experts in areas of policy making, law, strategy development, administration and enforcement. In this regard equal participation of industry professionals, academia and legal practioners are required. The major suggestions given by the policy makers in developing a national capacity in terms of IP are,

   - Strengthening of RGNIIPM, Nagpur which is a committed institute of Central Government towards national capacity building related to IP
   - Integration of IPR into the University level curriculum for all technical, management and medical courses. IPR shall also be integrated to all major training institutes (like Judicial academies and National Academy of Administration)
   - Institutes to have their own IP policy
   - Gradual introduction of IP teaching in schools and setting up of centers of skill development in educational institutions
   - Empowering women innovators through customized capacity building programmes.

CHAPTER 20

FAQ's

1. **Can a minor file a patent application?**

   Ans: Yes, a minor can also file a patent application. Section 6 of Indian Patents Act describes the eligibility of an applicant for filing an Indian patent application. The person filing a patent application must be the 'true and first inventor' of the invention or any person who has been assigned the rights by the so called 'true and first inventor' or can be any person who is a legal representative of a deceased 'true or first inventor'.

2. **What minimum educational qualifications are required for filing an Indian patent application?**

   Ans: No basic qualification is required for filing an Indian patent application. The person must be the true and first inventor or an assignee of the same, having the right to file a patent application

3. **What happens if the applicant dies after filing a patent application or after grant of patent?**

   Ans: A legal representative of the deceased who by law represents the estate of the deceased person can own the patent by applying to the Controller in prescribed Form. Thus, a patent can be inherited

4. **Is hiring a patent agent must for filing a patent application**

   Ans: Hiring a patent agent is not mandatory. The applicant can himself file a patent with Form 1 and Form 2 which are available on the Indian patent website

5. **Can a patent be filed in a group of multiple persons?**

   Ans: Yes, a patent can be filed either alone or jointly with many applicants and also jointly with any organization. It must be kept in mind that if all persons involved in filing the patent are natural persons, fee applicable is less. However, if any person jointly files an application with other organization, the fee applicable shall be high

6. **Who is the owner of the patent – applicant or inventor?**

   Ans: Applicant is the owner of the patent. The difference between applicant and owner is already explained in this book. If the applicant and owner are different, then it means that the inventor has assigned all rights to the applicant. This assignment of right by the inventor to the applicant is executed in Form 1.

7. **Do I have to visit the patent office for submitting my application?**

   Ans: NO, patent application can be filed through online mode using the e-filing system. The applicant has to procure a digital signature for using the e-filing mode.

8. **I have an Indian patent for my invention, can people of other countries use my invention without my consent**

   Ans: Patent is a territorial right, so an Indian patent is valid within the Indian jurisdiction. So, any people from other country can use the invention without the consent of the patentee. However, the product obtained from the said invention cannot be sold in India as the invention has been patented in India. Thus, if the patentee wants his invention to be protected in other countries, he has to file patent in all those foreign countries where he wants his invention to be protected

9. **I am a University student, if I file a patent who shall be the owner? Will my University help me financially to bear the expenditure of patenting process?**

   Ans: if any invention has taken place in a University and if the said invention has been carried out by a group of students under the mentorship of a University faculty using University infrastructure and funding, and if an active IPR policy is in place, then the patent applicant shall be the University, who will be the owner of the patent. According to the IPR policy of the University, the University shall bear the expenses incurred for patenting the invention. However, if no IPR policy exists, then the inventor can themselves file a patent in their own name and in such circumstances the University may not bear the expenditure involved in patenting the invention.

10. **What is the expenditure involved in filing an Indian patent application?**

    Ans: The actual expenditure depends upon the nature of the applicant. Fees for natural person filing a patent application is very less when compared to organizations filing a patent application, which is comparatively very high. The fee payable for natural person at the time of filing a patent application is Rs 1600 only. A fee of Rs 4000 has to be paid after publication of the application for the purpose of examination of the application. However, this fee for examination can also be paid at the time of filing the application. Noteworthy, to mention that once the patent is granted renewal fees every year has to be paid for keeping the patent active

11. **How will I understand if my invention is patentable or not?**

Ans: Section 3 of Indian Patents Act describes those inventions which are not patentable (explained in this book). An inventor can go through those descriptions to find out that if the said invention happens to fall under such category. Moreover, inventor may obtain search report to assess the patentability aspect of the invention before filing the application. Applicant can conduct his own search through Google patents, Espacenet (https://worldwide.espacenet.com/) or Indian patent database to find what type of closely similar inventions already exists. Search has to be conducted using specific keywords. Alternatively search report can be obtained from a patent agent on payment basis.

12. **If there are multiple applicants, then does the first applicant holds the maximum share for the patent?**

Ans: There is no such rule that the first applicant (in case of multiple applicants) holds the major credit of the patent. The order in which the applicants are named in the patent application does not signify anything. All the applicants are deemed to be considered having the same right unless a separate deed is executed by the applicants where the share of every applicant is mentioned. In the event of the patent being commercialized or licensed out, the revenue earned shall be shared among the applicants based on the percentage mentioned in the deed executed solely by the applicants before filing of the patent application. Such practice of assigning more weightage to the first author and corresponding author is practiced in publication of research papers, but the same is not applicable for patents.

13. **I have filed an Indian patent application, how can I track the progress of the application**

Ans: If you have filed an Indian patent application, its progress cannot be tracked until 18 months. After 18 months, the application is published and it can be searched from the Indian patent database. The Indian patent database shall reflect the real time status of your application once it is published.

14. **Do I have to present my working model or invention before the examiners of the Indian patent office?**

    Ans: No. Physical display of the invention before the examiners is not required. All details related to the working of the invention including experimental data, drawings and all such procedure by reading which a person skilled in the art can reproduce the invention, shall have to be presented in Form-2 while filing the patent application. The examiner shall study those explanations to come to a conclusion.

15. **What is meant by patent publication? What actually is published? Is it equivalent to a research publication?**

    Ans: After 18 months from the date of filing the patent application, the same is published in the patent office official journal. Only the abstract is published along with the names of the applicant/inventor, their address and other details regarding dates. This publication is just intimation to public regarding the subject matter of the filed patent, it cannot be considered to be equivalent to a research publication.

16. **My research partner has filed a patent application without my name and knowledge as well. I came to know about this matter when I saw the publication of the patent application on the internet. What shall I do now?**

    Ans: In such a case, anytime before the grant of a patent, you can file a pre-grant opposition in Form 7A along with evidence that you were also one of the partners of the research and some part of the research was wrongfully taken from you. You can even claim that you knew about the research before filing of the patent application and hence the subject matter lacks novelty. No fee is required for filing a pre-grant opposition. Written clarification shall be sought from the applicant regarding the charges alleged by you in the pre-grant opposition. However, if you come to know about this act after grant of patent, you can still file an objection as post-grant opposition but it has to be done within 1 year from intimation of grant in official journal. Fee is applicable for this purpose.

17. **I am a research scholar; I presented my research as oral/poster presentation in a seminar. Can I still file a patent application because many people present in the seminar have seen and listened to my research?**

    Ans: Yes, you can still file a patent provided you do so within 01 year from the opening date of such seminar. Presentation in seminar or in a exhibition does not constitute loss of novelty due to anticipation, if within 01 year the patent is filed from the date of such event

18. **I want to file a patent application online, but the submission portal is asking for digital signature for the purpose of registration of the applicant. Where can I get a digital signature**

    Ans: It is very easy to purchase digital signature online. Names of certain service providers are already mentioned in the patent website (also explained in this book). One such service provider is e-mudhra from whom digital signature can be procured through online. Aadhar card and pan card shall be required for placing the order for digital signature. Once the order is placed after filling certain information through online, the same shall be delivered within 4-5 days.

19. **What is the language for filing Indian patent application?**

    Ans: English or Hindi

20. **After filing a patent application, can I withdraw it?**

    Ans: Yes, patent application can be withdrawn anytime before the grant of patent. After filing, if the request for examination is not made within 48 months, the application is automatically considered to be withdrawn

21. **I can see several Forms on the website, but I am confused which forms I have to fill at the time submission of my patent application**

    Ans: You have to fill Form-1 which is the basic patent application form, Form-2 which is the heart of the application containing all details of the invention. These two forms are mandatory. Form-3 and Form-5 are also required but it is not mandatory to submit them at the time of application submission, as additional time is provided to submit them. Form-18 is the request for examination which can be filed at the time of application submission or at a later stage.

22. **I have received the first examination report, within how many days I have to file my reply**

    Ans: You have to file your reply within 6 months which is extendable by 3 months

23. **I don't have a law degree, can I become a patent agent?**

    Ans: Law degree is not necessary for becoming a patent agent. You must be a science graduate above 21 years of age

24. **After becoming a patent agent in India, can I practice in foreign country**

    Ans: No, you can practice only in India. For practicing in foreign country, you need to fulfill the criteria prescribed by that particular country

25. **I am interested to receive training in IPR. Whom to approach?**

    Ans: RGNIIPM, Nagpur is a Central Government institute committed towards capacity building in the field of IPR. Public training programmes are regularly arranged throughout the year. Please check their website for their training schedule. Registration fees could be approximately 10,000 for 5-6 days training programme.

26. **I am an ordinary common man and wants to file a patent application for my innovation. I do not know how to draft my application and complete other paperwork and neither do I have fund to hire a patent agent. Will the Government help me?**

    Ans: In such situation, you must approach the Patent Facilitation Centre (a Government office under Department of Science & Technology, New Delhi) of your state, they will help you in drafting the application and its submission.

27. **I have a brilliant idea of a project; can I patent my idea so that nobody else can use it?**

    Ans: Idea cannot be patented. You have to convert your idea into a product or process to file a patent

28. **I have received a project from a government funding agency. An invention takes place out of the said project. Do I have to take permission from the funding agency for filing a patent, will the filing expenditure be covered from the project?**

    Ans: Assuming that you could be a faculty working in an educational institution having its own IPR policy, in the above-mentioned case the University and the funding agency both becomes the joint applicants for the patent application. Permission from the funding agency and their involvement in the patent in the capacity of joint owner is mandatory. The cost of patent filing process can be utilized from the contingency amount of the project or from the overhead grant (if available and if permitted by the host University)

29. **I am an Indian research scholar and I want to use an Indian patent literature for my research work. Is it permitted or shall it constitute an infringement?**

Ans: Yes, you can use the patent literature for your Ph.D research which is likely to yield a degree. Infringement will take place if you develop something out of your research using the said patent literature and then start commercialization of the product which is likely to yield revenue. Patent literature can be used for educational and institutional research purpose likely to yield a degree.

30. **Do I have to renew my patent every year?**

Ans: Yes, you have to pay renewal fees annually for keeping the patent alive. Failure of payment of renewal fees will cause the patent to lapse and then others can start using your patent without causing any infringement.

Index

R

S

T

U

V

W

www.ingramcontent.com/pod-product-compliance
Lightning Source LLC
Chambersburg PA
CBHW080930240926
51849CB00003BA/422
9789391910174